26-03 BK Bud March 04

D1534687

For Reference

Not to be taken from this room

SOUTHEASTERN COMMUNITY
COLLEGE LIBRARY
WHITEVILLE, NC 28472

Ref.
D
843
.R46
2000

The Cold War
Collapse of Communism

by Earle Rice Jr.

For Reference

Not to be taken from this room

SOUTHEASTERN COMMUNITY
COLLEGE LIBRARY
WHITEVILLE, NC 28472

Lucent Books, San Diego, CA

Titles in the History's Great Defeats series include:

The Aztecs: End of a Civilization
The Cold War: Collapse of Communism
The Third Reich: Demise of the Nazi Dream
The British Empire: The End of Colonialism

No part of this book may be reproduced or used in any form or by any means, electrical, mechanical, or otherwise, including, but not limited to, photocopy, recording, or any information storage and retrieval system, without prior written permission from the publisher.

Library of Congress Cataloging-in-Publication Data

Rice, Earle.
  The Cold War : collapse of communism / by Earle Rice Jr.
    p.   cm. — (History's great defeats)
  Includes bibliographical references and index.
  Summary: Presents a history of the tense, often combative, relations between Soviet Russia and the United States from the end of World War II to the fall of communism in 1989.
  ISBN 1-56006-634-2 (alk. paper)
    1. Cold War—Juvenile literature. 2. World politics—1945—Juvenile literature. 3. Post-communism—Juvenile literature. [1. Cold War. 2. United States—Foreign relations—Soviet Union. 3. Soviet Union—Foreign relations—United States. 4. World politics—1945-] I. Title. II. Series.
D843 .R46   2000
327.47073—dc21

00-008311

Copyright © 2000 by Lucent Books, Inc.
P.O. Box 289011
San Diego, CA 92198-9011
Printed in the U.S.A.

Table of Contents

Foreword

ISTORY IS FILLED with tales of dramatic encounters that sealed the fates of empires or civilizations, changing them or causing them to disappear forever. One of the best known events began in 334 B.C., when Alexander, king of Macedonia, led his small but formidable Greek army into Asia. In the short span of only ten years, he brought Persia, the largest empire the world had yet seen, to its knees, earning him the nickname forever after associated with his name—"the Great." The demise of Persia, which at its height stretched from the shores of the Mediterranean Sea in the west to the borders of India in the east, was one of history's most stunning defeats. It occurred primarily because of some fatal flaws in the Persian military system, disadvantages the Greeks had exploited before, though never as spectacularly as they did under Alexander.

First, though the Persians had managed to conquer many peoples and bring huge territories under their control, they had failed to create an individual fighting man who could compare with the Greek hoplite. A heavily armored infantry soldier, the hoplite fought in a highly effective and lethal battlefield formation—the phalanx. Possessed of better armor, weapons, and training than the Persians, Alexander's soldiers repeatedly crushed their Persian opponents. Second, the Persians for the most part lacked generals of the caliber of their Greek counterparts. And when Alexander invaded, Persia had the added and decisive disadvantage of facing one of the greatest generals of all time. When the Persians were defeated, their great empire was lost forever.

Other world powers and civilizations have fallen in a like manner. They have succumbed to some combination of inherent fatal flaws or

4

disadvantages, to political and/or military mistakes, and even to the personal failings of their leaders.

Another of history's great defeats was the sad demise of the North American Indian tribes at the hands of encroaching European civilization from the sixteenth to nineteenth centuries. In this case, all of the tribes suffered from the same crippling disadvantages. Among the worst, they lacked the great numbers, the unity, and the advanced industrial and military hardware possessed by the Europeans. Still another example, one closer to our own time, was the resounding defeat of Nazi Germany by the Allies in 1945, which brought World War II, the most disastrous conflict in history, to a close. Nazi Germany collapsed for many reasons. But one of the most telling was that its leader, Adolf Hitler, sorely underestimated the material resources and human resolve of the Allies, especially the United States. In the end, Germany was in a very real sense submerged by a massive and seemingly relentless tidal wave of Allied bombs, tanks, ships, and soldiers.

Seen in retrospect, a good many of the fatal flaws, drawbacks, and mistakes that caused these and other great defeats from the pages of history seem obvious. It is only natural to wonder why, in each case, the losers did not realize their limitations and/or errors sooner and attempt to avert disaster. But closer examination of the events, social and political trends, and leading personalities involved usually reveals that complex factors were at play. Arrogance, fear, ignorance, stubbornness, innocence, and other attitudes held by nations, peoples, and individuals often colored and shaped their reactions, goals, and strategies. And it is both fascinating and instructive to reconstruct how such attitudes, as well as the fatal flaws and mistakes themselves, contributed to the losers' ultimate demise.

Each volume in Lucent Books' *History's Great Defeats* series is designed to provide the reader with diverse learning tools for exploring the topic at hand. Each well-informed, clearly written text is supported and enlivened by substantial quotes by the actual people involved, as well as by later historians and other experts; and these primary and secondary sources are carefully documented. Each volume also supplies the reader with an extensive Works Consulted list, guiding him or her to further research on the topic. These and other research tools, including glossaries and time lines, afford the reader a thorough understanding of how and why one of history's most decisive defeats occurred and how these events shaped our world.

A Shadow of
Introduction Uncertainty

A specter is haunting Europe—the specter of communism.
—Karl Marx, *Manifesto of the Communist Party*

IN THE WANING DAYS of World War II, the United States, the Soviet Union, and their respective allies, entered into a period of armed hostility that cast a shadow of uncertainty over international relations, underlined with the ever-present threat of a nuclear cataclysm. This era of doubtfulness and distrust between the Western and Eastern powers became known as the Cold War. The identifying phrase was coined in 1947 by Herbert Bayard Swope, a well-known newspaper writer and editor of the time, in a speech written for financier and presidential adviser Bernard Baruch.

This so-called Cold War stands alone as the longest-running and most-gripping suspense drama of the twentieth century. Arguably, it began in 1945, commencing with the inability of the wartime allies to reach agreement on the independence of Poland, on the reunification of Germany, and on the division of Europe as a whole. The Cold War dragged on for forty-four anxiety-ridden years, threatening several times to erupt into a "hot" war—or even to destroy the world in a nuclear catastrophe—before U.S. president George H. W. Bush and Soviet president Mikhail S. Gorbachev officially pronounced it over on December 2, 1989.

On Christmas Day 1991, little more than two years after the end of the Cold War, Gorbachev resigned as president and chief of state of the by-then-defunct Soviet Union. The Soviet Union had officially dissolved with the creation of the Commonwealth of Independent

6

States (CIS) seventeen days earlier. Gorbachev's resignation effectively marked the end of the Soviet empire and the collapse of communism in Europe. From the vantage point of elapsed time, the Soviet experiment with communism appeared fated to fail from the start. The Cold War guaranteed that it did.

Causes of Communism's Collapse

The causes of communism's collapse in the Soviet Union were numerous and varied, as were the 15 union republics, the 20 autonomous (self-governing) republics, 8 autonomous provinces, 10 autonomous districts, and the 6 regions and 114 other provinces that united to form the Union of Soviet Socialist Republics (USSR). But in a very basic sense, the factors contributing most to the fall of the Marxist ideology and the consequent dissolution of the Soviet Union can be reduced to four: the insane arms race; communism's basic flaw (the system had no means of economic calculation, and its inability to determine what it could afford and balance outlay against expected income inevitably led to its failure); the rise of ethnic nationalism within the unitary structure

U.S. president George Bush and Soviet president Mikhail Gorbachev meet on the eve of announcing the official end of the Cold War in 1989.

of the USSR; and finally, governmental reforms (glasnost, or openness, and perestroika, or restructuring) that were intended to strengthen the Communist Party and preserve communism but instead hastened both the breakup of the party and the collapse of the system.

There were, of course, many additional factors in the failure of communism and the breakup of the Soviet Union, such as: a one-party totalitarian government that operated with savage efficiency in time of war or social upheaval but ultimately became a heavy brake on the wheel of national development; a ponderous bureaucracy that perpetuated myths of a great society of workers and was turning its citizens into single-dimensional beings; the deprivation of religious and civil rights; the senseless incursion into Afghanistan; and so on. Yet none of these self-destructive elements brought greater weight to bear on the underpinnings of the Communist system than the aforementioned four factors, which accordingly have been selected for closer examination.

The arms race, communism's basic flaw, the rise of ethnic nationalism, and governmental reforms played starring roles in a modern-day political drama in which the specter of communism was banished from Europe. Under the shadow of unrelenting uncertainty, these four critical factors performed daily for more than four decades in the theater of the Cold War.

Chapter 1 The Cold War

The Americans could not understand that it was of little avail to win the war [World War II] strategically if we lost it politically.

—Field Marshal Bernard L. Montgomery,
commander of British forces in Europe, 1945

"From Stettin in the Baltic to Trieste in the Adriatic, an iron curtain has descended across the Continent [of Europe]."[1] So spoke British statesman Winston Churchill in an address on international affairs at Westminster College in Fulton, Missouri, on March 5, 1946. Churchill was referring to an unseen barrier of secrecy and censorship that isolated the Soviet Union and its Communist satellites after World War II. (Soviet satellites were small nations that were politically or economically dependent on the Soviet Union, such as Czechoslovakia, Hungary, and other Eastern European nations, and thus adhered to Soviet policies.) Churchill's phrasing of *iron curtain* gave name to one of the most recognized and enduring symbols of what would soon become universally known as the Cold War. Many historians believe that his speech at Fulton lent formal public recognition to the start of the Cold War.

Origins of the Cold War

Some theorists point to the origins of the Soviet Union and the beginnings of the Cold War as being mutually inclusive events. They hold that Soviet Russia had waged a cold war (as opposed to a "hot"

9

or shooting war) against the United States since 1917. For example, George F. Kennan, a distinguished American statesman and ambassador to the Soviet Union in 1952, points out,

> There seems to be a widespread impression in this country that the Cold War, as something signifying a state of sharp conflict and tension between the two governments, began only in 1945, after the Second World War. This impression is erroneous. Never were American relations with Russia at a lower ebb than in the first sixteen years after the Bolshevik seizure of power in 1917.[2]

The Bolsheviks, members of the extremist wing of the Russian Social Democratic Party led by Vladimir Lenin, seized power in Russia on November 7, 1917. The new rulers of Russia vowed at the outset to spread their Marxist (Communist) doctrine throughout the globe and aimed at world domination. Thus, insist many observers, the Cold War began with the Russian Revolution of 1917.

A second opinion contends that the origin of the Cold War dates back only to the days immediately following the Yalta Conference. The conference was held in several villas near the Crimean resort town of Yalta from February 4 to 12, 1945. It marked the second and final

A military band leads a victory parade shortly after the Bolshevik seizure of power in 1917.

meeting of the Big Three Allied leaders who had guided their respective nations through most of World War II: President Franklin D. Roosevelt of the United States, Prime Minister Winston Churchill of Great Britain, and Premier Joseph Stalin of the Soviet Union. The conference dealt with a broad range of unresolved questions, particularly a four-power occupation of Germany (with France being the fourth power); plans for forming the United Nations (UN)—an international organization dedicated to preserving world peace—later in the year; the Soviet Union's agreement to enter the war against Japan; and a Soviet guarantee of a representative form of government in Poland.

Churchill, who was well known for his distrust of Soviet intentions, had wanted to coordinate Anglo-American policy in advance of the meeting. But Roosevelt purposely blocked Churchill's efforts in this regard. According to American diplomat William Averell Harriman, the president did not wish to "feed Soviet suspicions that the British and Americans would be operating in concert."[3]

Later, at Yalta, when the three leaders broached the subject of Poland, Roosevelt agreed to a Soviet proposal for subsequent elections in which "all democratic and anti-Nazi parties shall have the right to take part." But he did not support a British demand for international supervision of the voting. Instead, Roosevelt countered with his own Declaration on Liberated Europe, a proposal containing vague commitments espousing "the right of all peoples to choose the form of government under which they will live."[4]

Since Roosevelt's ambiguous declaration contained more rhetoric than substance, the Soviets were most pleased to sign it. Moreover, Roosevelt's stunning announcement of his intentions to withdraw all American troops from Europe within two years revealed precisely what Stalin most wanted to know. The supreme ruler of the Soviet Union did not wait long to act on the information.

On March 23, at a meeting of a commission established at Yalta to implement free elections in Poland, Soviet foreign minister Vyacheslav Molotov chillingly announced that the Polish elections would be conducted Soviet-style. Western officials interpreted this to mean Soviet-controlled elections—in other words, elections manipulated to ensure the outcome desired by the Soviets. When Roosevelt received Harriman's account of the meeting two days later, he banged his fist on the arm of his wheelchair. "We can't do business with Stalin," he said. "He has broken every one of the promises he made at Yalta."[5]

This realization came too late to the ailing president, who died quietly at his home in Warm Springs, Georgia, on April 12. His death came less than a month before Germany's unconditional surrender to the Allies. Despite Roosevelt's staunch wartime leadership, many of his detractors claim that it was his inept handling of the Allied negotiations at Yalta that opened the door to future Soviet expansion. This opinion is no longer widely shared, but some conservative critics continue to blame him for the onset of the Cold War.

Although students of the Cold War still debate the time of its origins, most observers would agree that it did not generate wide public awareness or concern until those uneasy years immediately following World War II. It was then that the struggle for a new world order began in earnest between two emerging superpowers, with Premier Joseph Stalin charting the course for the Soviet Union and President Harry S. Truman guiding the destiny of the United States.

The Truman Doctrine

Vice President Truman succeeded President Roosevelt upon the latter's death in April 1945 and took over the difficult task of bringing

Churchill, Roosevelt, and Stalin meet at Yalta in 1945. Some historians believe that the Cold War began after Stalin broke the promises he made at the Yalta Conference.

World War II to a speedy conclusion. Nor did his problems
cease with victory and peace.
He next had to grapple with
ways of dealing with the defeated nations and with means
of helping newly freed peoples. In 1945 he had to assume
a key leadership role in founding the United Nations. At the
same time, he faced the formidable task at home of restoring
his nation to a peacetime economy. And early in 1947, his
problems abroad took on a
new dimension.

In 1947 President Truman issued the Truman Doctrine, declaring the United States's opposition to communist expansion.

In February 1947 Britain
informed the United States
that it would be forced to dis-
continue its aid to Greece and
Turkey on March 31. Alarmed that Greece and Turkey might fall under Soviet influence, Truman successfully appealed to a joint session
of Congress on March 12 for $400 million to aid the two countries.
At the same time, and of far greater importance for the future, Truman drew a sharp distinction between two worlds in opposition—
one of free institutions, the other of terror and oppression. The
president asserted, "I believe that it must be the policy of the United
States to support free peoples who are resisting attempted subjugation by armed minorities or by outside pressures."[6]

Truman's declaration amounted to a sweeping U.S. commitment
to the free world with no limitations of time or place. It became
known as the Truman Doctrine and led to the U.S. policy of contain-
ment, a global ideological crusade against communism. "By presenting aid to Greece and Turkey in terms of ideological conflict between
two ways of life," observed historian John Lewis Gaddis, "Washington officials encouraged a simplistic view of the Cold War" that re-
stricted American diplomacy and "may well have contributed to the
perpetuation of the Cold War."[7]

Four Stages of the Cold War

The Cold War, in the popular view, is generally separated into four stages or time periods: from 1945 to 1953, from 1953 to 1962, from 1962 to 1973, and from 1973 to 1989.

In the first stage, both sides adopted irreconcilable positions and ceased to communicate with each other. This stage climaxed with the Korean War (1950–1953).

Following Stalin's death on March 5, 1953, U.S.-Soviet relations underwent a "thawing-out" period during the second stage, when the two sides began talking again. But the Cuban Missile Crisis in 1962 thrust the world to the brink of a nuclear war. A compromise agreement resolved the U.S.-Soviet confrontation and ended the second stage.

The Vietnam War dominated the third stage of the Cold War and led both military behemoths to advocate limiting the acquisition of strategic arms as a way of revitalizing their declining economies.

As the two superpowers entered into the fourth and final stage of the Cold War in 1973, their mutual economic needs fostered a period of détente (a relaxing of tensions), while U.S. president Richard M. Nixon (and later Presidents Gerald Ford and Jimmy Carter) engaged in arms-control talks with Soviet secretary general Leonid Brezhnev. But détente ended abruptly when the Soviets invaded Afghanistan in 1979, and U.S.-Soviet relations again turned cold. They remained cold until Soviet leader Mikhail Gorbachev's proposals for disarmament and democratic changes in Eastern Europe lifted the iron curtain and ended the Cold War in 1989.

The Marshall Plan

The first stage of the Cold War is generally considered to have begun in 1945 with the world divided into two camps, one led by the United States, the other by the Soviet Union. From 1945 to 1948, the Soviet Union expanded its original sphere of influence to include the Communist-governed nations of Hungary, Romania, Poland, and Czechoslovakia in its camp. The Soviets had occupied Bulgaria in 1944 and a Communist dictatorship that aligned itself with Moscow was established there in 1946. Although Yugoslavia—under the Communist regime of Marshal Josip Broz Tito—declared itself a nonaligned nation, it usually sided with the Soviet Union in matters of East-West disagreement.

In June 1948 the United States announced the European Recovery Program—popularly named the Marshall Plan after U.S. secretary of state George C. Marshall—to aid in the postwar rehabilitation of twenty-two European nations. The plan continued for three years and eventually cost American taxpayers $10.2 billion.

In an attempt to counter the Marshall Plan's influence in its own sphere, the Soviet Union introduced the Council for Mutual Economic Assistance, or Comecon, in January 1949. Initially, Comecon's purpose was to boost trade among member nations in the Eastern bloc, but its membership was extended in later years to include other nations, such as Vietnam and Cuba. Comecon offered far less aid than the Marshall Plan and consequently was less successful. Even so, the council lasted until the collapse of the Eastern European Communist regimes during 1989–1990.

Fearful that the Soviets might construe his plan as a U.S. attempt to further its influence in Europe, Marshall publicly declared, "Our policy is directed not against any country or doctrine but against hunger, poverty, desperation and chaos."[8] Marshall's declaration seemingly fell on deaf Soviet ears, as the first clash of the Cold War erupted shortly thereafter. That clash was over the fate of Germany.

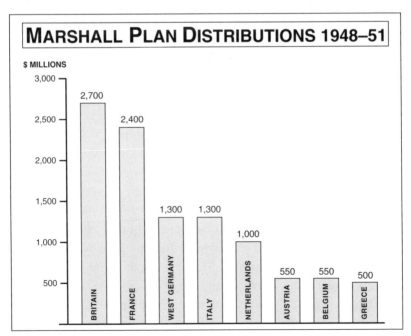

MARSHALL PLAN DISTRIBUTIONS 1948–51

The Berlin Blockade and Airlift

At the end of World War II, the Allies divided Berlin (like Germany as a whole) into four zones—the American, British, French, and Soviet sectors—to facilitate military control by their occupation forces. Geographically, Berlin stood as an oasis 110 miles inside the Soviet-occupied zone.

By June 1948 inflation was soaring in Germany. After failing to reach agreement with the Soviets on how to curb it, the Western powers, acting on their own, introduced a new deutsche mark (the basic monetary unit of Germany) into their zones on June 18. The Soviets, fearing that an improved economy in West Germany would jeopardize their control of East Germany, responded by issuing their own new mark on June 23.

At the same time, the Soviets shut off electricity to the Western zones and stopped all deliveries of coal, food, milk, and other supplies. The next day, all traffic—both land and water—between West Berlin and the West stopped. With the city completely blockaded, the Soviets declared that all rights of the Western powers to administrate Berlin were no longer valid.

The Truman administration viewed the Soviet blockade as a major test of the West's will to defend the freedom of not only West Berlin but also all of Western Europe. Open war, or at least a serious confrontation, between the East and the West loomed very close at hand. But cool heads in the West acted swiftly to organize an unprecedented airlift into West Berlin.

The airlift to preserve freedom lasted for almost a year, with supply-laden aircraft landing at the rate of one a minute, delivering four thousand tons of supplies a day to the isolated city and transforming it from the capital of a defeated fascist power into an icon of courageous resistance to totalitarianism. Years later, in 1961, President John F. Kennedy described Berlin as "a showcase of liberty, a symbol, an isle of freedom in a communist sea."[9] From the Soviet perspective, Berlin stood as a clear demonstration of the West's resolve to resist Communist expansion. Moscow began rethinking its policies toward the status of Berlin and the two Germanys.

The Soviets finally hinted that they were prepared to reopen discussions on the question of German reunification. On May 5, 1949,

Berlin children cheer as an American plane brings food and other supplies to their blockaded city.

the four occupying powers signed an agreement that ended the crisis after almost eleven months, but not before sixty American and British pilots had lost their lives during the airlift and participating nations had expended more than $200 million (in 1949 dollars). Nor did East and West reach any agreement on German reunification.

The North Atlantic Treaty of 1949

In the meantime, with the airlift still ongoing, the Western Allies responded to fears inspired by the Soviet blockade and signed an agreement establishing a new alliance, the North Atlantic Treaty Organization (NATO), on April 4, 1949. It was the third of three prime U.S. foreign policy legacies of the Truman administration (along with the Truman Doctrine and the Marshall Plan) and the first Cold War organization to transcend Europe. Its original members consisted of the United States, Canada, and the Western European nations, except for Sweden, Switzerland, and Spain. The aim of NATO was explicitly defensive, as indicated by the following extract from Article 5 of the North Atlantic Treaty of 1949:

> The Parties agree that an armed attack on one or more of them in Europe or North America shall be considered an attack against them all and they consequently agree that, if such an armed attack occurs, each of them, in exercise of the

right of individual or collective self-defense recognized by Article 51 of the Charter of the United Nations, will assist the Party or Parties so attacked by taking forthwith, individually [or] in concert with the other Parties, such action as it deems necessary, including the use of armed force, to restore and maintain the security of the North Atlantic area.[10]

The establishment of NATO symbolized the solidarity of Western European and North American nations against the spread of communism, and it signaled a departure from the isolationist policies traditionally exhibited by the United States. By further widening the increasingly broad schism between the Soviet Union and the Western powers, it also gave rise to a new German state. As an additional bulwark against further attempts by the Soviets to expand their influence in Germany, the NATO powers supported the creation of the Federal Republic of Germany (West Germany) from the three Western zones of occupation in May 1949. The creation of West Germany galvanized the Soviet Union's already strong antagonism toward the West.

In October 1949 the Soviets answered the Western Allies by orchestrating the creation of a second new German state in the Soviet occupation zone, the German Democratic Republic (GDR, or East Germany). The iron curtain shifted farther west and henceforth followed along the border of the divided German states.

Beyond the alienating effects that the creation of NATO and the division of Germany exerted on U.S.-Soviet relations in 1949, an event of far greater significance occurred that summer. On August 29, 1949, Soviet scientists successfully detonated a nuclear device. A nuclear capability that until then had belonged solely to the United States was now shared by its Cold War antago- nist. This shared capability led both sides to enter into an arms race that held the world hostage to the threat of nuclear annihilation for several decades.

The Korean War

The first test of whether the world's two nuclear powers could exercise restraint in the use of nuclear force came in 1950, at the end of the Cold War's first stage, when a "hot" (shooting) war erupted in Korea. On June 25, with the approval and encouragement of Joseph Stalin, the Soviet- equipped armies of Communist North Korea swept across the border into non-Communist South Korea. The North Koreans planned to re- unify Korea under the Communist regime of Kim Il Sung.

Korea had been temporarily divided at the close of World War II to facilitate its occupation. The Soviets and the Americans respec- tively occupied the territories north and south of the dividing line at the thirty-eighth parallel. In 1948, the division of Korea became per- manent with the formation of the People's Republic of Korea (North Korea) and the Republic of Korea (South Korea), accompanied by the withdrawal of Soviet and U.S. forces.

The North Korean armies quickly captured the South Korean capital of Seoul in an unprovoked attack that U.S. secretary of state Dean G. Acheson regarded as "an open, undisguised challenge to our internationally accepted position as the protector of South Korea, an area of great importance to the security of American-occupied Japan."[11] The world waited anxiously to learn how President Truman would meet the latest Communist challenge.

Truman immediately authorized U.S. naval and air forces to as- sist the South Koreans. On June 30 he ordered U.S. ground troops into action. The war to contain communism, which Truman dubbed a "police action," was fought under the banner of the United Nations, but the United States supplied far and away the largest share of troops and war matériel.

In November 1950, as UN troops under the overall command of U.S. general Douglas MacArthur neared the Yalu River that sepa- rates North Korea from the People's Republic of China, Chinese troops entered the war and forced the UN troops to withdraw to the thirty-eighth parallel. The war remained stalemated for the next two and one-half years. It ended in a cease-fire on July 27, 1953. (A formal peace agreement has never been signed.) The not-so-cold Cold War had now spread to Asia, as the Chinese and the Soviets vied with each other for the leadership of the Communist world.

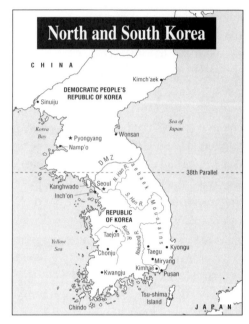

Despite the stalemate in Korea, President Truman, and later President Dwight D. Eisenhower, refrained from expanding the action into the People's Republic of China or from using nuclear weapons to win the war. Their restraint in the use of nuclear arms established a precedent that all nations, so far, have perpetuated.

The Eisenhower Years

As the Korean War dragged on, President Truman's popularity waned and he decided not to seek reelection. General Dwight D. Eisenhower, who had led the Allied forces to victory in Europe during World War II, won election as U.S. president in 1952, partly on his campaign promise to end the fighting in Korea.

At the beginning of the second stage of the Cold War, Eisenhower's veiled threats to escalate the war, possibly with nuclear weapons, coupled with the death of Soviet dictator Joseph Stalin, persuaded the Chinese that it was in their best interests to end hostilities in Korea. Stalin, unknown to Americans at the time, had insisted on the war's continuance. Upon Stalin's death on March 5, 1953, his successors allowed the Korean peace talks to reach a cease-fire agreement.

Cold War tensions lessened for a time after the Korean cease-fire, but they built up again during the Suez Crisis of 1956. The crisis erupted when the United States withdrew its promised financial support for building Egypt's Aswan Dam on the Nile River. In retaliation, Egyptian president Gamal Abdel Nasser nationalized the Suez Canal, which provoked a joint British, French, and Israeli military venture to overthrow Nasser's regime. The Soviet Union threatened to rush "volunteers" to aid Nasser, but the crisis was quickly resolved by U.S.-sponsored UN resolutions to call off the attackers. Nasser afterward welcomed a Soviet presence in the Middle East.

In response to the threat of Soviet involvement in the Middle East, President Eisenhower asked Congress for funds to provide economic aid to Middle Eastern countries, and for the authority to use armed force in the region. Later known as the Eisenhower Doctrine, the president's answer to the Soviets declared that the United States would defend the Middle East against "overt armed aggression from any nation controlled by International Communism."[12]

The Warsaw Pact

During the third year of the Eisenhower administration, the remilitarized Federal Republic of Germany (West Germany) was formally integrated into NATO on May 9, 1955. The Soviets responded quickly. On May 14 the Soviet Union formed its own alliance with the Eastern bloc—the Soviet-dominated Communist nations of Eastern Europe consisting of Albania, Bulgaria, Czechoslovakia, East Germany, Hungary, Poland, and Romania. The Soviet answer to NATO became known as the Warsaw Pact and was headquartered in Moscow.

Soviet-directed strategic planning for the Warsaw Pact nations anticipated an attack by five NATO army groups and targeted a wide array of NATO installations for retaliatory strikes. Thus two alliances now faced each other, separated by an iron curtain. But at least one critical difference set them apart: NATO membership was strictly voluntary and its senior partner, the United States, could not arbitrarily impose its will or preferred strategies on the other member nations; disagreements occurred routinely within NATO, lessening its cohesion and effectiveness. Conversely, the Soviet Union controlled the Warsaw Pact nations with an iron hand, and Moscow dictated all strategy to the extent that at times member nations did not know what was expected of them.

Fortunately for Europe and the world, NATO and Warsaw Pact strategies have never clashed on the battlefield. But the Soviets invoked provisions of the Warsaw Pact to provide a formal basis for their intervention in civil revolts against communism in Hungary in 1956 and again twelve years later in Czechoslovakia in 1968.

As might be expected, the Soviets quickly condemned the Eisenhower Doctrine. The People's Republic of China echoed the Moscow line, suggesting that the publicly declared Soviet-Chinese solidarity, which had shown signs of weakening, remained firmly in effect. Eisenhower's unilateral action moved U.S. leaders closer to Israel and to despotic allies such as the shah of Iran, which, in turn, led to the oil embargoes of the 1970s, followed by the Iranian revolution and an intense hatred of the United States in some parts of the Middle East.

During the last years of the Eisenhower administration, a coalition of Democratic politicians, defense contractors, and Pentagon officials began claiming that Eisenhower had allowed the U.S. arsenal of intercontinental ballistic missiles (ICBMs) to lag behind that of the Soviets, thereby creating a serious missile gap.

On October 4, 1957, the Soviet Union's launching of *Sputnik I*—the world's first artificial satellite—seemed to lend credence to the charges of a Soviet missile lead. (A missile powerful enough to launch a satellite into orbit could clearly deliver warheads to targets in the United States.) In the early 1960s, newly accumulated U.S. intelligence data proved the charges to be false. In the meantime, however,

A Soviet woman displays a model of Sputnik I, *the first artificial satellite.*

U.S. policymakers called for massive defense spending to close a missile gap that had already overwhelmingly favored the United States.

In President Eisenhower's farewell address in 1961, he cautioned the nation to "guard against the acquisition of unwarranted influence, whether sought or unsought, by the military-industrial complex."[13]

The Cuban Missile Crisis

The rapid buildup of U.S. missiles in the late 1950s carried over into the administration of President John F. Kennedy in the early 1960s. According to some Cold War observers, the U.S. missile buildup became the chief factor in Soviet leader Nikita Khrushchev's decision to install medium- and intermediate-range ballistic missiles in Cuba in an attempt to level the nuclear playing field. Thus, in the autumn of President John F. Kennedy's second year in office, the earth moved to the brink of nuclear extinction.

On October 14, 1962, a routine flight of an American U-2 photoreconnaissance plane over Cuba spotted the presence of Soviet surface-to-surface missiles capable of launching a nuclear strike against the United States. President Kennedy demanded their removal and imposed a naval blockade of the island. As people everywhere held their breath for thirteen fearsome days, diplomacy of the highest order succeeded in resolving the world's first nuclear showdown behind the scenes, with both sides making concessions to avert disaster.

Summing up the confrontation, U.S. secretary of state Dean Rusk later observed, "We were eyeball to eyeball, and I think the other fellow blinked."[14] That blink gave pause for the two superpowers—and the world at large—to reflect on the dire and irrevocable consequences of a nuclear war. The Cuban Missile Crisis ended the second stage of the Cold War. A hot war loomed just ahead.

The Vietnam War

Soviet military commanders viewed the Cuban Missile Crisis as a humiliation, and many government hard-liners began pressing for a massive arms buildup. Over the objections of some Soviet soft-liners, who wanted to spend less money on arms and more on economic development, the Soviets launched an escalated arms buildup that was to last well into the 1980s. As an adviser to Soviet leader Leonid Brezhnev later explained, "The remaining members of the

Hanoi residents walk through the rubble in front of their homes after surviving a bomb attack by the United States.

Politburo [political bureau; the policy-making and executive com-mittee of the Soviet Communist Party] simply decided not to inter-fere with military matters."[15]

Meanwhile, in the late 1950s and early 1960s, Presidents Eisen-hower and Kennedy began sending increasing numbers of military ad-visers to South Vietnam to help thwart an attempt by Communist North Vietnam to overthrow the South Vietnamese government of Ngo Dinh Diem. President Lyndon B. Johnson, Kennedy's successor, greatly in-creased U.S. support to more than a half million troops by 1969.

The Soviets were at first reluctant to become involved in the Southeast Asian conflict. But when U.S. planes bombed the North Vietnamese capital of Hanoi, the Soviets decided to extend military aid to a "fraternal socialist country."[16] Moscow began by sending surface-to-air missiles to defend North Vietnam but declared hands-off to involvement in South Vietnam.

In all, the USSR supplied Hanoi with $1.5 billion in military aid, complemented by some $670 million provided by Communist China.

These sums paled in comparison to the $112 billion spent by the United States in South Vietnam. The war in Vietnam bled the United States and cost the lives of more than fifty-eight thousand Americans. In the end, it was the Soviet Union that gained prestige as the noble defender of a small Third World nation attempting to fight against the domination of a foreign aggressor.

The conclusion of major American involvement in Vietnam in 1973 marked the end of stage three and the start of stage four of the Cold War. The two superpowers now continued to explore a period of détente—an interval of relaxed tensions between them that had begun in the late 1960s.

Détente

Over the Cold War's four-plus decades of alternating freezes and thaws, a détente in U.S.-Soviet tensions occurred several times. But the term particularly belongs to the 1970s, in the era of negotiations between U.S. president Richard M. Nixon and Soviet general secretary Leonid Brezhnev. Their negotiations included the Strategic Arms Limitation Talks (SALT), the Basic Principles Agreement (a code of international conduct), and the Helsinki Accords (an East-

President Nixon and Brezhnev successfully negotiated several détentes in U.S.-Soviet tensions during the 1970s.

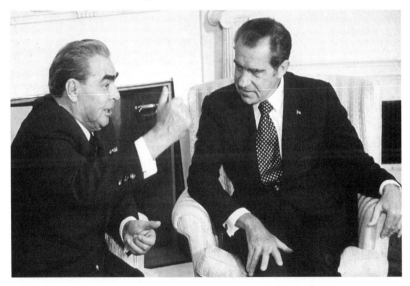

West agreement on the postwar national boundaries of Eastern European countries). More than a decade of détente ended in the early
1980s, when the Soviet invasion of Afghanistan, dissent in Poland,
further escalation of the arms race, and President Ronald W. Reagan's aggressive anti-Soviet stance—not least his introduction of the
Strategic Defense Initiative (SDI, or Star Wars)—all combined to re-
freeze U.S.-Soviet relations.

The Last Thaw

The final thaw in relations between the two superpowers came after
Mikhail S. Gorbachev won election as general secretary and Soviet
leader in 1985. Gorbachev, who also became Soviet president and
chief of state in 1988, faced a rapidly deteriorating economy when he
took office and tried to liberalize and revitalize Soviet socialism and
society. His well-intentioned policies of glasnost (openness) and perestroika (restructuring) resulted in the death of Soviet communism, the
collapse of the Soviet Union, and the end of his own political career.

*Mikhail S. Gorbachev,
seen here after assuming
office of general secretary
and Soviet leader in 1985,
dramatically changed the
political direction of his
country.*

Gorbachev did not foresee these events when he embarked on his reforms. He had intended to streamline communism, not kill it; to strengthen the USSR, not dissolve it; and to lead his nation to prosperity and a respected place in the sun, not plummet from the heights of leadership in failure.

The West will long remember and admire Gorbachev for his statesmanship and for promoting freedom in his own nation and in the Soviet satellites. Yet at home, any admiration his own people felt toward him quickly turned to dislike and distrust when his domestic policies failed to improve their lot and lifestyle. In sum, he gambled on innovation and openness to solve the myriad problems confronting his ailing nation. And he lost. He might have won his gamble had it not been for the unbearable weight of the arms race.

Chapter 2 The Arms Race

The arms race strained the very sinews of the [Soviet] com-
mand economy, and brought closer the approaching crisis of
the entire system.

—Dmitri Volkogonov, former defense
adviser to Soviet president Boris Yeltsin

T HE INCESSANT FINANCIAL DRAIN of the arms race on the Soviet
economy ranks high on the list of causes for the collapse of
communism and the resultant dissolution of the Soviet Union.
The Soviets spent untold billions of dollars on armaments that might
have been far better spent improving their ailing economy and the
lifestyle of their impoverished people. It should be mentioned that
the United States emerged from World War II with the world's rich-
est economy. Although it similarly spent enormous sums during the
arms race, it did so without severely impinging on the high standard
of living of the average American. Such was not the case with the average Soviet citizen. But in the absence of Soviet fiscal accountability during the Cold War, the actual cost of the arms race and the true
extent of its crippling effect on the Soviet economy cannot be mea-
sured with total accuracy. Nor can the start of the arms race between
the United States and the Soviet Union be dated without fear of con-
tradiction. But it seems safe to say that the origins of the U.S.-Soviet
arms race extend at least as far back as the early 1940s.

On November 6, 1942, Lavrenty Beria, head of the Soviet
NKVD (secret police), informed Soviet supreme ruler Joseph Stalin

of a matter of grave importance: "Research has begun in the capitalist countries [the United States and Britain] on the use of atomic power for military purposes."[17] Research in the West was directed toward harnessing the enormous power of the atom to make a bomb. Beria went on to describe the stage this research had reached and recommended the establishment of a scientific advisory body, under his direction, to study, coordinate, and direct work on the evaluation and strategic application of atomic energy.

Stalin, excited over the possibilities of a new atomic weapon, replied, "Can't we speed it all up to use in the war against the fascists [the Nazis and their allies]?"[18]

Stalin's elation soon subsided when a memorandum from Soviet nuclear physicist Igor Kurchatov stated, "Soviet research on the problems of uranium [an element providing a source of nuclear energy] is considerably behind the English and Americans."[19]

Kurchatov recommended that a large group of physicists first be assigned to study the problems of uranium. Stalin complied, ordering a special laboratory built with the job of producing a hundred tons of uranium in 1944–1945.

In late 1945, after the United States had demonstrated the world's first atomic bombs at Hiroshima and Nagasaki in August,

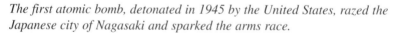

The first atomic bomb, detonated in 1945 by the United States, razed the Japanese city of Nagasaki and sparked the arms race.

Stalin ordered Beria to develop a Soviet bomb by 1948. In early 1946, Stalin summoned Kurchatov to his office in the Kremlin. With Beria looking on, he told the physicist that atomic work must advance swiftly "on a broad front, on a Russian scale, and that in this respect all possible help will be provided."[20]

Working in close harmony, Beria and Kurchatov created a special design bureau and constructed secret cities (as the United States had done) to house a host of designers brought together for the task. Beria and his scientists failed to deliver a bomb by Stalin's 1948 deadline. But on August 29, 1949, at a remote testing site in Semipalatinsk, Kazakhstan, the Soviets detonated their first nuclear device, a plutonium bomb. Code-named "First Lightning," it was almost an exact replica of the bomb the United States had exploded over Nagasaki.

Beria shouted with joy at their success, hugging and kissing Kurchatov, unable to contain himself. He knew too well how Stalin rewarded failure. "It would have been a great misfortune if it hadn't worked,"[21] he said. Everyone present knew what he meant. Beria's life had literally hung in the balance since 1945.

A Milestone

In 1945 the U.S. Joint Chiefs of Staff (JCS) had estimated that it would take Stalin at least five years to develop a bomb, probably because it had taken the United States about three. But a consensus of Western intelligence in 1949 favored mid-1953 as the most likely earliest date for a Soviet bomb. At that time, no one in the West realized how much the Soviets had profited by espionage.

American atomic secrets supplied to the Soviets in 1944 and 1945 by the married couple Julius and Ethel Rosenberg were particularly useful to the Soviets. The Rosenbergs were subsequently convicted of espionage in a controversial trial and executed on June 19, 1953, with many supporters still protesting their innocence. Despite their disavowal of guilt, telling evidence against the Rosenbergs—compiled from deciphered Soviet espionage messages but understandably not revealed in the trial—came to light afterward.

Some years later, Soviet leader Nikita Khrushchev ended most speculation as to the couple's guilt or innocence when he revealed, "I heard from both Stalin and [Soviet foreign minister Vyacheslav]

Molotov that the Rosenbergs provided very significant help in accelerating the production of our atomic bomb."[22]

With the explosion of the Soviet atomic bomb, it was clear that the United States no longer held a monopoly on the threat of nuclear annihilation. And for lack of a better milestone, the U.S.-Soviet arms race can now be said to have begun with a flash of "lightning" at Semipalatinsk.

A "Window of Strategic Advantage"

In 1950, President Harry S. Truman approved the development of the hydrogen bomb—a thermonuclear weapon vastly more powerful than an atomic bomb. U.S. scientists conducted the first successful

Policy Departure

Historical sources vary widely as to precisely when the Cold War began. Some historians feel that it began with a letter written by President Harry S. Truman to U.S. secretary of state James F. Byrnes on January 5, 1946. The president later described this letter in his memoirs as "the point of departure of our policy." In this excerpt from Martin Walker's *The Cold War,* Truman discusses the U.S. postwar policy toward the Soviet Union.

At Potsdam we were faced with an accomplished fact and were by circumstances almost forced to agree to Russian occupation of eastern Poland, and that part of Germany east of the Oder river by Poland. It was a high-handed outrage. There isn't a doubt in my mind that Russia intends an invasion of Turkey and the seizure of the Black Sea Straits to the Mediterranean. Unless Russia is faced with an iron fist and strong language, another war is in the making. Only one language do they understand—"How many divisions have you?" I do not think we should play compromise any longer. We should refuse to recognize Rumania and Bulgaria until they comply with our requirements; we should let our position on Iran be known in no uncertain terms . . . and we should maintain complete control of Japan and the Pacific. We should rehabilitate China and create a strong central government there. We should do the same for Korea. Then we should insist on the return of our ships from Russia and force a settlement of the Lend-Lease debt [U.S. material aid to the Soviets in World War II] of Russia. I'm tired of babying the Soviets.

A huge billowing mushroom cloud rises into the atmosphere after the detonation of a hydrogen bomb at Enewetak Atoll in 1952.

test of a hydrogen (fusion) bomb at Enewetak Atoll in the western Pacific Ocean on November 1, 1952. The bomb's blast generated five hundred times the energy of the bomb dropped on Hiroshima.

In 1954, the United States successfully tested an H-bomb that could be delivered by long-range aircraft. By the mid-1950s, the U.S. arsenal of long-range bombers capable of delivering nuclear bombs on targets in the Soviet Union included the Consolidated B-36, the largest warplane ever built, and the Boeing B-52.

On November 9, 1955, only three years after the first successful U.S. test of a hydrogen bomb, the USSR detonated its own H-bomb. It yielded some 1.6 megatons (1 megaton = 1 million tons). Significantly, the Soviets airlifted the bomb to its target and exploded it at an altitude of several thousand feet. Earlier in the year, at their May Day 1955 air show, the Soviets had displayed a prototype of a long-range bomber, the heavy turbo-prop Bear (Tupilev Tu-95). By late 1955, the Soviets possessed a thermonuclear capability, but they would also soon own the means to deliver H-bombs on targets in the United States.

From the birth of the A-bomb until the mid-1950s, the United States had held what renowned U.S. strategist Norman Friedman calls a "window of strategic [nuclear] advantage"[23] over the Soviets. That window slammed shut when the Soviets launched *Sputnik I* in 1957 and abruptly turned the arms race into a missile chase.

The Missile Chase

On October 4, 1957, the Soviet Union, under First Secretary Nikita Khrushchev, orbited *Sputnik I*—the earth's first artificial satellite. The world looked on in amazement at the technological achievement of a nation whose people had until then been considered backward at best. Stunned U.S. observers were nevertheless quick to recognize the strategic implications of the Soviet feat: A rocket large enough and powerful enough to boost a satellite into orbit could also carry nuclear warheads to U.S. cities. The missile chase was on. Writes Norman Friedman,

> The race to build and deploy the first ICBMs was probably the closest the Cold War ever got to an arms race between the superpowers. Between about 1955 and 1960, both tried to build much the same kind of weapon. At all other times during the Cold War one side generally built weapons while the other, for a wide variety of reasons, did not. Even the missile race was not the action-reaction situation so often imagined. Both sides realized at about the same time that they wanted ICBMs, and each pursued its goal knowing very little about what the other side was doing.[24]

In the sense that weapons development on both sides underwent periodic starts and stops, Friedman may be correct in assessing that the arms race rarely constituted a race at all. On the other hand, both superpowers did compete in a deadly game of arms one-upmanship throughout the Cold War, as each side attempted to outstrip—or simply to achieve parity with—the other.

During most of the 1950s, for example, the United States relied primarily on long-range bombers to deliver nuclear payloads on target, particularly the Boeing B-52. The B-52 Stratofortress, powered by eight jet engines mounted in podded pairs, first flew in 1952 and entered service with the U.S. Strategic Air Command (SAC) in 1955. It attains a top speed of about 640 miles per hour (mph) and can cruise some 8,300 miles without refueling.

The United States's extensive arsenal during the Cold War included the B-52 Stratofortress bomber.

Although initially and primarily intended to carry nuclear bombs, in later years the B-52 served as a conventional bomber in the Vietnam War in the 1960s and 1970s, and again in the Persian Gulf War in 1990, capable of delivering more than twenty tons of bombs. Later models, the B-52Ds, were refitted to carry air-to-surface missiles (cruise missiles and decoy missiles). The long-lived, long-range bomber remained in service into the twenty-first century.

In 1956 the Myasishchyev M-4 (or Mya-4, code-named "Bison" by NATO) entered the Soviet air service. The M-4, a four-engine strategic bomber patterned after the B-52, reached a maximum speed of 560 mph and a range, when fully loaded, of about 5,000 miles. It could carry four nuclear bombs or a conventional bomb load of some sixteen tons. Clearly, its capabilities fell short of the B-52's. Rather than engage the United States in a costly bomber race, however, Soviet leader Nikita Khrushchev decided to concentrate the nation's economic resources on the design and development of intercontinental ballistic missiles.

Although the Soviets' successful launching of *Sputnik I* in 1957 highlighted Soviet advances in rocket science, the missile chase (or race) had actually begun in 1946, when both the United States and the Soviet Union imported German rocket experts to work on their respective weapons and space programs. German scientists and engineers had created the V-2 rocket for use against England during the final months of World War II and led the way in the field of ballistic missilery. (A ballistic missile is so named because it does not use wings or other aerodynamic surfaces for lift; rather, it follows a trajectory according to the laws of ballistics—like an artillery shell—when its thrust dissipates.)

The Americans developed the first ICBM—the Atlas—in the early 1950s. But by 1955, the Soviets were mass-producing the SS-3, an intermediate-range ballistic missile (IRBM). And in 1957 the Soviets successfully launched their first ICBM over a range of five thousand miles, using the same rocket engine that had lofted *Sputnik I* into orbit. From 1960 onward, with both sides trying to outdo the other, they each developed the capacity of launching ballistic missiles from submarines. And each superpower produced a wide array of shorter-range missiles and a broad variety of battlefield nuclear weapons.

The Soviet Union shows off its military might by showcasing an ICBM during a 1965 military parade in Moscow.

On October 17, 1961, in an address to the Twenty-second Communist Party Congress, Khrushchev reported on the success of the Soviet hydrogen-bomb program and added, "The re-arming of the Soviet Army with nuclear missile technology [is] fully complete. Our armed forces now have weapons powerful enough to enable them to crush any aggressor."[25] Khrushchev failed to mention the huge costs of the missile program in his address, which ultimately bore much of the responsibility for the pitifully substandard living of the average Soviet citizen.

During 1956–1957, in an effort to raise the Soviet standard of living and lessen the strain of the arms race on the quivering Soviet economy, Khrushchev had advocated a policy of peaceful coexistence with the United States. During a brief détente with the West he reduced his arms expenditures from $29.5 billion in 1955 to $26.7 billion in 1956. Even with a slight increase to $27.6 billion in 1957 spending remained well under 1955 levels. Even though the United States spent $31.9 billion more than the Soviet Union on defense over the same two years, however, the far richer U.S. economy was still able to sustain a much higher standard of living for Americans.

From 1960 to 1969, U.S. defense spending totaled about $605.6 billion, compared to $621.9 billion by the USSR. Much of this spending was applied to the missile chase. The astronomical sums expended by both sides ensured that the ICBM would become the enduring symbol of the 1960s.

Nuclear Arms Control

As the two superpowers entered the 1970s, their ongoing game of one-upmanship now encompassed much of the globe as each nation strived to spread its own influence—or negate that of its rival—by creating alliances and proffering military and economic aid to emerging Third World (underdeveloped or undeveloped) nations in both hemispheres. Early in 1970, for instance, one observer noted,

> The United States had more than 1,000,000 soldiers in 30 countries, was a member of four regional defense alliances and an active participant in a fifth, had mutual defense treaties with 42 nations, was a member of 53 international organizations, and was furnishing military or economic aid to nearly 100 nations across the face of the globe.[26]

Five years earlier, in May 1965, U.S. secretary of state Dean Rusk argued, "This has become a very small planet. We have to be concerned with all of it—with all of its land, waters, atmosphere, and with surrounding space."[27] By the 1970s, as evidenced by its alliances, treaties, and burgeoning aid to overseas nations, the United States was clearly showing its concern for the planet. Although the Soviets projected far less power and influence around the globe during the first two and one-half decades of the Cold War, their efforts to exert their will in North Korea, Egypt, Iraq, Indonesia, India, Cuba, Angola, North Vietnam, and elsewhere added huge costs to the already overburdened Soviet economy.

In 1974, for example, the USSR spent $109 billion on defense, against a U.S. defense expenditure of $85 billion. The well-equipped Soviet armed forces numbered 3 million personnel, compared to U.S. armed forces of 2 million. Both superpowers possessed 5,000 combat aircraft and, with a total warship tonnage of 2.1 million tons, the Soviet navy yielded only .7 million tons to the U.S. Navy's 2.8 million tons. More important at the time, however, the USSR had by then surpassed the United States in sheer numbers of nuclear delivery vehicles—ICBMs, IRBMs, SLBMs (submarine-launched ballistic missiles), and medium- and long-range bombers—by a margin of 3,835 to 2,213. But the United States made up for the numerical deficit with superior design and technology (better guidance controls and systems reliability), wider weapons deployment, less vulnerable launch sites, and so on.

The delicate balance resulting from the Soviet numerical advantage and the American technical superiority created a nuclear standoff between the two superpowers in the 1970s, dictated by the strategic principle of "mutually assured destruction" (MAD). Optimists of the day preferred to lend a more reassuring cast to the acronym, interpreting it as "mutually assured deterrence." In any case, the impasse highlighted the need for some form of nuclear arms control.

Brezhnev and Détente

On May 26, 1972, U.S. president Richard M. Nixon and Soviet premier Aleksey Kosygin signed the SALT I (Strategic Arms Limitation Treaty I) agreement in Moscow. (Although the United States, the Soviet Union, and Great Britain, which had become a nuclear power in

President Nixon approved the development of the Trident, a submarine–launched cruise missile, shortly after signing the SALT I agreement.

1957, had agreed in a series of earlier treaties to limit—and later to cease—nuclear testing and to stop the spread of nuclear weaponry, nothing existed to limit the size or restrict the growth of their nuclear arsenals.) Both superpowers regarded SALT I as the first step toward nuclear parity. But concerned that parity would not be maintained, Nixon took immediate steps to thwart any future Soviet advantage.

President Nixon approved the development of two new weapons that he felt could be deployed within the five-year term limit of SALT I: the cruise missile (air- and sea-launched, or ALCM and SLCM) and the submarine-launched Trident missile. He also authorized a longer-term plan for developing a new heavy missile (MX) whose design would stress accuracy and striking power. Nixon probably saw these new weapons (which later held enormous significance in optimizing U.S. military strength and options) as insurance against any Soviet breach of strategic arms limitations.

Similarly, under the collective leadership of Premier Aleksey Kosygin and First Secretary Leonid Brezhnev, the Soviets took steps of their own to guard against any attempt by the United States to subvert the arms agreement. Since SALT I limited ICBMs but not IRBMs, the Soviets speedily enhanced their IRBM stockpile by using

SALT I and SALT II

On May 26, 1972, U.S. president Richard M. Nixon and Soviet premier Aleksey Kosygin, consummating talks that had begun in 1969, signed the Strategic Arms Limitation Treaty I (SALT I) in Moscow. The SALT I agreement, scheduled to run for five years, set limits on various kinds of nuclear delivery systems. It also limited the deployment of Soviet antiballistic missiles (ABMs). Both signatories regarded the treaty as the first step toward continuing future negotiations.

The treaty left the USSR with 2,358 intercontinental ballistic missiles (ICBMs) and the United States with 1,710; the USSR with 62 submarine-launched ballistic missiles (SLBMs), the U.S. with 44. Not everyone in the U.S. camp supported this seeming imbalance. But the U.S. Senate—recognizing that the United States still possessed more accurate and reliable ICBMs, more advanced nuclear submarines and better SLBMs, more and heavier bombers, superior multiple independently targetable reentry vehicle (MIRV) technology, more warheads, and Allied bases around the Soviet Union—felt obliged to ratify the treaty in the name of strategic parity between the two nations.

Continuing negotiations between the two superpowers in the 1970s produced a period of relaxed tensions. The détente led to SALT II, an agreement calling for equality in nuclear delivery vehicles—2,250 for each nation, including MIRVs. On June 18, 1979, U.S. president Jimmy Carter and Soviet first secretary Leonid Brezhnev signed the treaty at a meeting in Vienna. But the U.S. Congress refused to ratify the treaty when Soviet forces invaded Afghanistan at year's end.

the upper and lower (without the middle) stages of their mobile ICBM as an IRBM, the Pionir (SS-20).

At the same time, Brezhnev ordered a very expensive buildup of Soviet ground forces that might be needed to implement a newly devised plan to overcome NATO forces in the event of a conventional war in Europe. (During the Brezhnev period, Soviet defense spending placed an enormous strain on the Soviet economy, averaging about 14 to 15 percent of the Soviet gross national product (GNP) compared to some 6 to 7 percent of the richer U.S. GNP allocated for defense spend-

Brezhnev's Legacy

Leonid Brezhnev's rule of eighteen years, the longest of any Soviet leader after Stalin, ended with his death on November 10, 1982. History will remember the decade of détente during his term in office. But history will equally recall his regime for cronyism, corruption, and its failure to address the need for economic reform during what is often referred to as the Soviet "period of stagnation."

Nor will history forget Brezhnev's brutal suppression of Czech dissent with Warsaw Pact troops and tanks during the "Prague Spring of 1968" campaign. His swift action came in response to Czech leader Alexander Dubcek's attempts to initiate democratic reforms. Brezhnev later justi-

Brezhnev's term was marked by a period of economic stagnation.

fied his use of force, declaring that the USSR was duty bound to intervene, irrespective of national boundaries, wherever socialism was threatened by attempts to restore capitalism. His declaration became known as the Brezhnev Doctrine.

Brezhnev's legacy for the 1980s constituted a Soviet economy burdened by inefficiency, shortages, and a growing technology gap—an economy that could ill afford the defense expenditures that the Brezhnev regime had imposed on it. Brezhnev's demise also left contentious issues pending with the United States: a turbulent labor movement in Poland, arms control, trade relations, human-rights and emigration questions, Soviet involvement in Afghanistan, and Soviet-supported Vietnamese occupation of Cambodia.

ing over the same time frame.) The Soviet army grew dramatically from 90 motor rifle divisions (plus 50 tank and 7 airborne divisions) in 1965 to 110 motor rifle divisions in 1974, 134 in 1983, and 150 in 1987.

Despite the ongoing arms buildup on both sides, U.S.-Soviet relations softened during the 1970s, as the danger and expense of the arms race became increasingly apparent to politicians in Washington and Moscow. During this period of détente, U.S. president Jimmy Carter and Soviet first secretary Brezhnev came to terms on SALT II—a second arms-limitation agreement—in June 1979. But the U.S. Congress rejected it when the Soviets invaded Afghanistan in December 1979. The Soviet aggression marked a somewhat official end to a decade-long détente under Brezhnev. In truth, however, détente had already faded.

Doomed to Fail

A long period of economic stagnation, followed by Soviet adventurism in Afghanistan, left the Soviet economy in shambles and U.S.-Soviet relations at a low ebb. Two days after Leonid Brezhnev's death on November 10, 1982, Yuri V. Andropov, a longtime head of the KGB (Soviet intelligence agency and heir to the NKVD), won election as general secretary. What appeared to both Soviet and Western observers alike to be the beginning of a promising new era of Soviet reforms ended almost before it began with Andropov's death on February 9, 1984.

The Communist Central Committee elected Konstantin U. Chernenko as Andropov's successor. In his inaugural address to the committee, Chernenko declared that "the system of economic management and our whole economic mechanism are in need of serious restructuring." [28] Nevertheless, Chernenko turned away from needed reform and allowed a return to cronyism, bribery, and other corruptions that characterized his short thirteen-month tenure as little more than an extension of the Brezhnev era. Chernenko died on March 10, 1985. A rising star on the Soviet political horizon had already been groomed to replace him: Mikhail Sergeyevich Gorbachev.

Meanwhile, half a world away, Ronald Wilson Reagan had assumed office as the fortieth president of the United States in January 1981. He had campaigned on promises of rebuilding U.S. defenses and restoring self-esteem and national pride to all Americans. Reagan quickly became the West's most outspoken critic of the Soviet

Union, which he scathingly termed "the evil empire" and immediately initiated a massive military buildup.

In 1983 President Reagan proposed the Strategic Defense Initiative (SDI), popularly known as Star Wars. This proposal called for the development of a great defensive shield capable of destroying incoming enemy missiles. The president viewed the SDI as a force for peace and publicly offered to share the system with the Soviets, once achieved, as a sign of his sincerity. But a furious Yuri Andropov denounced Reagan's initiative.

By denying the USSR a retaliatory capability, Andropov fumed, strategic defense represented nothing more than "a bid to disarm the Soviet Union." He warned that the Reagan administration was "continuing to tread an extremely dangerous path" and was asking for nuclear war. "This is not just irresponsible, it is insane."[29] Insane or not, research on Star Wars moved forward. American engineers, scientists, and technicians worked on the Strategic Defense Initiative for ten years without producing an operational system, but the initiative's enormous costs were not a total loss.

Two years after the Cold War's conclusion, in 1993, former Soviet foreign minister Alexander Bessmertnykh disclosed to a group of former U.S. and Soviet officials that, because of the SDI, Soviet military officials had demanded better missiles, adding still more weight to the buckling Soviet defense budget. At the same time, the prospect of the SDI had enabled Soviet government officials opposed to the Cold War to advance arms-control agreements. In these ways, at least, Star Wars played a role in ending the Cold War.

The arms race effectively ended when President Ronald Reagan and General Secretary Mikhail Gorbachev signed the Intermediate-Range Nuclear Forces (INF) Treaty in a meeting held in Washington, D.C., during December 7–10, 1987. The INF Treaty called for eliminating stocks of intermediate-range missiles with nuclear warheads. It was the first agreement to not only limit the growth of nuclear weaponry but also to reduce the size of existing nuclear arsenals.

The world welcomed the reduction of weaponry wrought by the INF Treaty, but the arms race represented only one of many problems that had been facing Mikhail Gorbachev since his election as Soviet general secretary on March 11, 1985. Gorbachev soon recognized that the Soviet Union was eroding away from within and was near

Gorbachev and Reagan sign the historic INF Treaty, ending the decades-long arms race.

collapse. "Just like reformers before me, I thought that we had a system that could be improved," he revealed years later. "Instead, I learned that we had a system that needed to be replaced."[30] The end of the insane arms race and Gorbachev's well-intentioned reforms came too late to save the USSR.

The Soviet experiment with communism was doomed to fail from the beginning. It failed not because of the Cold War and the arms race; they were merely symptoms of a greater malady. In the end, the Soviet experiment failed simply and inevitably because of communism's basic flaw.

Communism's
Chapter 3 Basic Flaw

The proletariat [the working class] needs state power, a central-
ized organization of force, an organization of violence, both to
crush the resistance of the exploiters and to lead the enormous
mass of the population—the peasantry, the petty-bourgeoisie
[the lower middle class] and the semi-proletarians—in the work
of organizing a socialist economy.

—Vladimir Ilich Lenin

O N NOVEMBER 7, 1917, the Bolsheviks overthrew the existing
government of Nicholas II, the last czar of Russia. Five years
later, on December 30, 1922, the Bolsheviks-turned-Russian-
Communists founded the Union of Soviet Socialist Republics (USSR).
For the next sixty-nine years, the Soviet Union sought to overthrow capitalism around the world. But capitalism held fast against the onslaught
of Soviet communism, and the Soviet Union ultimately collapsed from
within, largely because of an inherent flaw in its Communist philosophy.

Unlike capitalism, Soviet communism was not an economic system but rather a political one that controlled every aspect of Soviet
life. Totalitarian in nature and practice, its application generated
great wealth for the few and poverty and squalor for the masses—the
antithesis of what the Communist revolutionaries had promised. This
economic imbalance resulted in part from corruption in high places
(which in time might have been rectified), but also from the inalter-
able fact that communism lacked the one indispensable element of
any vibrant economy: plain old business sense.

44

An economy's successful operation relies on knowing the cost of everything—raw materials, equipment and machinery, building space, labor, inventory, overhead, shipping and handling, and much more. The success of any business venture depends on the ability to know and control costs so that expected (and real) profits exceed production expenses. Communism's basic flaw is that it lacked the means for calculating and regulating the cost/profit margin.

This was largely because of the manipulation of expense figures to suit the aims of whatever Soviet dictator was in power. Such manipulations allowed the Communist bureaucrats to claim economic progress when in reality the true state of the economy became hidden not only from the Soviet citizenry but also from the manipulators themselves. In addition to such corruptions, financial accountability was often hindered further by the ever-burgeoning maze of Soviet government and

The Soviet Experiment

In November 1917 the Bolsheviks, led by Vladimir Ilich Lenin, overthrew the existing government of Czar Nicholas II. The Bolsheviks became the Russian Communist Party in 1918. By the spring of that year, the Communists had transferred some five hundred enterprises to state management.

By 1921, after suppressing all rival political groups, the Communists proved exceptionally adept at coercion and dictatorial practices. But they exhibited far less skill at managing production and consumption—as time and a string of fiscal failures would painfully reveal.

On December 30, 1922, the Communists founded the Union of Soviet Socialist Republics (USSR, or Soviet Union), the first government in world history to call itself socialist. Communism had triumphed. But communism's triumph signified only the beginning of a long, agonizing experiment that would torment the Russian soul for the next seven decades, only to end in defeat in 1991.

Revolutionary leader Vladimir Lenin.

economic institutions. One hand, literally, did not know what the other was doing. And unlike the U.S. government—with its system of checks and balances among its executive, legislative, and judicial branches—the Soviet government answered only to itself.

The Soviet Economy

Under the Soviet system, the state owned all land, minerals, and buildings. It limited private ownership to such personal property as household and personal-care items, automobiles, financial assets, and homes (although most city living spaces were rented). In certain instances, the state granted limited access to (but not ownership of) land plots for gardening or constructing private dwellings.

The economic system adhered to the basic methods and priorities established by Joseph Stalin: central planning, militarization, and heavy industry. The Council of Ministers set broad economic policies and priorities. It controlled several agencies, most importantly Gosplan, the state planning agency, and Gosbank, the central bank. The central plans reflected the hopes of the planners but how the system actually functioned fell far short of the plans' goals. Failures over the years were masked behind a screen of falsified statistics while a succession of five-year plans gave the illusion of continuing production successes despite diminishing growth rates and missed deadlines.

Unknown to the Soviet public and the outside world, the Soviet military and nuclear sectors were consuming more than 30 percent of the nation's gross national product (GNP). Soviet heavy industry deluged the nation with a torrent of unwanted and unneeded iron, steel, and chemicals. And Soviet agriculture, though capable of producing huge amounts of low-grade food, could not deliver it to the family table because of inadequate means of transportation. In the final analysis, the economy produced huge quantities of tanks, aircraft, and rockets, but failed to meet the basic needs of its people.

Under communism, the true costs of Soviet production were not known; the government determined supply without regard to demand and set wages and prices arbitrarily; labor was forced. Thus, there was no competition for jobs, and workers labored without incentives for achievement or prospect of advancement. Most important, the government was never held accountable for its fiscal irresponsibilities and thus gradually drifted into financial insolvency.

The Soviet Government

To govern themselves, the Soviets introduced a unique system of two governments operating in parallel: the Communist Party of the Soviet Union (which held the true power) and the formal constitutional government (which functioned as an instrument of the party). The only important constitutional clause, according to Norman Davies in *Europe: A History*, was the one delegating "the leading role" to the Communist Party. This simple passage rendered all other provisions of the constitution, and all other Soviet laws, subject to the interpretation of the party and its officials.

Separate but parallel party and state hierarchies were established for the USSR in its entirety, and for each of the republics (except for the Russian republic, which used a coordinating bureau) as well as for provinces, districts, and large cities. The Central Committee met mandatorily at intervals of six months and bore the major burden of party work. Three agencies—whose members were formally named by the Central Committee (but preselected in private)—sat in perpetual session: the Politburo, the Secretariat, and the Commission of Party Control.

The Politburo, or political bureau, in fact created the Central Committee—and thus national policy—and directed its activities; the Secretariat, wherein lay the real power, handled most of the party's administrative work and appointed officials to execute party policy at lower levels; and the Commission of Party Control enforced the fulfillment of party policies.

At the bottom of the hierarchy, party membership was assembled into primary groups often called cells, which were organized in villages, collective farms, factories, schools and universities, and elements of the armed forces.

The Communist Party of the Soviet Union governed with exclusive power until its monopoly was rescinded in 1990. A year later, both the Soviet Union and the party dissolved.

Such were the winds that filled the sails of a Soviet ship of state sailing unswervingly toward economic disaster and spreading disillusionment, discontent, and dissent in its wake. The Soviet experiment with communism was a voyage of discovery in uncharted waters and dense fog. Without an economic compass to guide its passage, the Soviet ship was doomed from the start to run aground on the shoals of fiscal irresponsibility.

"Stalinist Totalitarianism"

The ill-fated course of Soviet communism has sometimes been characterized as "the mistake of Columbus." Martin Malia, a professor of history at the University of California at Berkeley and a recognized authority on Russian history, explains the allegory:

> The [Communist] Party set sail for the spice-perfumed isles of Socialism but ended up, by the late 1930s, on the impassable continent of Stalinist totalitarianism and its offshore Gulag Archipelago [a reference to the Soviet corrective labor camps]—quite an achievement no doubt, but not precisely what the crew had in mind on enlistment. Like Columbus, the Party never realized just where it had landed, but insisted to the end that its "soviet power" was indeed "real socialism."[31]

Joseph Stalin, born Iosif Vissarionovich Dzhugashvili, took over the helm of the Soviet ship of state when Lenin fell ill in 1922. Elected general secretary of the Central Committee of the Communist Party, Stalin (named after the Russian word *stal*, meaning "steel") shaped the course of the Soviet Union's destiny until his death in 1953.

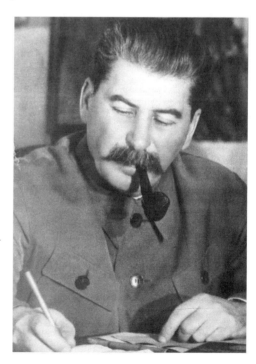

Joseph Stalin's unrelenting drive for a Soviet-controlled world cost millions of Soviet lives and the near economic collapse of the country.

Under Stalin's rigid steerage, the winds of change that billowed the sails of his ship of state were sixfold and interrelated, beginning with central planning and extending through accelerated industrialization, collectivized agriculture, rearmament, ideological warfare, and political terror. Stalin launched the first of a series of five-year plans in October 1928, overseen by Gosplan. In 1931 Stalin told his managers, "We are fifty or a hundred years behind advanced countries. We must make good this distance in ten years. Either we do so, or we will go under."[32]

The first five-year plan (announced in 1928) was aimed at creating "the second America" (that is, a prosperous nation with a high standard of living) and was based on achieving an annual industrial growth of 20 percent for five straight years. How unrealistic this goal was can be seen by noting that previous U.S. growth rates had never surpassed 8.7 percent. Valerian Kuibyshev, the regime's chief economist, tried desperately to make the statistics reflect Stalin's fantasy targets, but in a scribbled note to his wife, he was forced to concede, "I can't balance it out."[33]

Carved in stone, Kuibyshev's words might have served as an epitaph for countless millions of Soviets who died trying to deliver on Stalin's demands. Stalin achieved many of his industrial and agricultural goals at a ghastly cost in human lives—lives that might have helped to fashion a prospering economy had they been properly utilized.

In 1928 the industrial growth-rate index stood at 111 percent of its 1911 level; by 1938 it had soared to 658 percent. Soviet industrialization was achieved by producing more and consuming less, which at the laboring level simply meant working harder and eating less. Absolute priority was given to the steel, power, coal, and chemical industries. Quality lagged far behind quantity. Cost versus profit accountability was routinely rigged to serve Stalin's ends or lost in the maze of compartmentalized Soviet bureaucracies.

"Falsified statistics," writes historian Norman Davies, "became the object of an official cult whose central temple stood in the Permanent Exhibition of Economic Achievement in Moscow."[34] Stalin surrounded himself with statisticians who could fashion any data to fit his objectives.

Doctoring statistics posed no problem for Stalin's rearmament program, however, for it was conducted in secrecy under a special separate budget, the very existence of which was publicly denied until 1989. A Soviet-style military-industrial complex flourished from 1932 onward, as Stalin modernized the Soviet army with tanks, aircraft, parachute troops, and more. Arms spending weighed heavily on the Soviet ship of state, as it plowed slowly but unerringly toward the rocks and shoals of the "impassable continent of Stalinist totalitarianism."

The Foundation of Soviet Life

In 1929 Stalin ordered the collectivization of agriculture, which had operated under Lenin's New Economic Policy (NEP) during most of the 1920s. During the transition from capitalism to socialism (1921–1928), the NEP had permitted some forms of capitalism to continue outside the purview of state control. Peasants, for example, were allowed to sell their grain in the marketplace after paying an assigned tax. Under Stalin's system of collective farms, the state assumed ownership of everything.

In 1932–1933, wealthy farmers known as kulaks resisted collectivization. Stalin acted swiftly to quell their dissent. By expropriating much of the nation's grain and exporting it to the world market at reduced prices, he created an artificial famine that merged with a natural famine to ravage the countryside and take the lives of some 5 million people by starvation.

In 1941 the Soviet economy approached total collapse when the German armies of Adolf Hitler captured the USSR's main industrial and agricultural regions in a matter of months. Out of obvious necessity, Stalin temporarily abandoned Soviet plans to export communism and exhorted his underfed and overworked population to form "a single war camp"[35] to fight the Great Patriotic War. The Soviets staved off both defeat and starvation and were instrumental in the defeat of Germany, although at a cost of some 24 million Soviet lives.

At war's end, Stalin initiated a determined effort to establish Soviet dominance in Europe and impose communism on the world. Through various political purges and strong-arm coercions, he maneuvered Eastern European governments under the umbrella of communism and controlled them from Moscow. He almost touched off a third global war with his blockade of Berlin in 1948–1949. And his obstructionist policies in the United Nations and in other Allied

Farmers march with their rakes raised in protest of Stalin's policy of collectivization of farms.

councils continually blocked efforts among nations to establish an enduring peace in the postwar world.

Stalin died on March 5, 1953, with the spread of the Communist ideology that began with Karl Marx and Friedrich Engels well underway. Both Marx and Engels believed that communism's success was tied to its adoption by workers abroad and called for them to unite. Vladimir Lenin echoed their belief and promoted some capitalist policies solely to buy time for the workers of the world to unite. "We never flattered ourselves with the hope that we could reach the end without the aid of the international proletariat,"[36] he said in a speech to the Third Congress of Soviets.

Lenin, as the first Communist ruler of Russia, exerted a great influence over its future in the twentieth century. He believed that a totalitarian government was needed to ensure a successful transition from capitalism to communism. He further believed that "once the majority of the people *itself* suppresses its oppressors, a 'special force' for suppression *is no longer necessary*. In this sense the state *begins to wither away.*"[37]

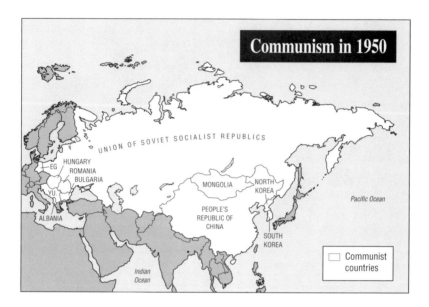

Under Stalin, the totalitarian state did not "wither away," of course, it grew steadily stronger. Yet in fairness—and despite his brutal excesses—it must be said that it was Stalin who stabilized Soviet communism and laid the foundation of Soviet life that was to endure until 1991.

A Task Too Great

Four days after Stalin's death, his embalmed body was laid to rest next to Lenin's in Moscow's Red Square. Georgi M. Malenkov succeeded Stalin as Soviet premier but was soon discredited by first secretary Nikita Khrushchev and forced to resign in favor of Nikolai A. Bulganin. Khrushchev, in turn, forced Bulganin from office in 1957 and replaced him as premier to become head of both the state and the party.

Nikita Khruschev, who has been variously portrayed by observers as ebullient, talkative, tough, shrewd, sociable, and earthy, described himself as "a man of the earth, of specific tasks, of coal, metal, chemistry, and, to a certain extent, of agriculture."[38] A self-confident man of tremendous energy, he gambled heavily in both foreign and domestic affairs. He openly declared his intentions of overtaking the United States in productivity and of helping to spread communism around the globe.

In February 1956, during an address to the twentieth Communist Party Congress, Khrushchev denounced Stalinism and scorned the

terror and atrocities under Stalin's long rule. The chief importance of
his speech, as Khrushchev noted later in his memoirs, "was that it
touched off the process of purifying the Party of Stalinism [known as
'de-Stalinization'] and re-establishing in the Party those Leninist
norms of life for which the best sons of our country had struggled."[39]
While castigating Stalin, Khrushchev failed to observe that Stalinism
grew out of Leninism, whose fundamental principle was unrestrained
class violence.

Khrushchev inherited the Cold War from Stalin and tried to ease
East-West tensions through a policy of peaceful coexistence. But the
reach of Khrushchev's unrealistic economic policies and ideological
desires far exceeded his grasp. "Khrushchev himself displayed an inability to distinguish between his own ideological hopes and real
economic possibilities," writes Tim McDaniel, a professor of sociol-
ogy at the University of California at San Diego. "Hero-socialists
could still, in his view, perform any task."[40] But they could not.

Khrushchev's policies failed both at home and abroad. In October 1964 a Kremlin coup removed him from office and sent him into
retirement. In the Soviet view, three key factors led to his dislodging:
economic reversals resulting from repeated crop failures; his defeat

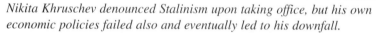

*Nikita Khruschev denounced Stalinism upon taking office, but his own
economic policies failed also and eventually led to his downfall.*

in the Cuban Missile Crisis (his forced withdrawal of Soviet missiles from Cuba); and an ideological dispute with China over the spread of communism that split the world into two Communist factions.

While riding the crest of a fleeting economic upsurge and a wave of technical achievements in the arms and space races, Khrushchev had once boasted that the Soviet Union would overtake the United States within twenty years. "We will bury you [economically],"[41] he vowed. But neither the boastful Khrushchev nor the creaking Soviet economy proved equal to the task, and a new pilot stood forth to guide the Soviet ship of state.

Soviet Stagnation

During the eighteen-year rule of Leonid Brezhnev that followed Khrushchev's downfall, the new Soviet first secretary proved himself to be a shrewd politician who recognized the consequences of altering the course of a sinking ship in midocean. After a brief, failed flirtation with economic reforms at home, with his partner Premier Aleksey Kosygin, Brezhnev spurned any further rocking of the boat on his watch and steered the state vessel straight into the economic doldrums.

While Brezhnev fostered a period of détente with the West during his term, his country endured a period of economic decline.

First Secretary Brezhnev (and later general secretary and marshal of the Soviet Union) shared the Soviet leadership with Premier Kosygin, but it soon became clear that Brezhnev had become first among equals. Brezhnev left most domestic matters to Kosygin while concentrating himself on conducting foreign affairs and strengthening the Soviet armed forces at the expense of a struggling Soviet economy. Under Brezhnev's leadership, troops from the Soviet Union and other Eastern European nations invaded Czechoslovakia in 1968, and Soviet troops invaded Afghanistan in 1979. During the intervening years, Brezhnev cultivated a decade of détente with the West. But at the same time he was busily exporting communism and supporting multibillion-dollar annual bailouts of Communist regimes in Angola, Cuba, Nicaragua, Vietnam, and elsewhere.

Brezhnev died in Moscow on November 10, 1982, two years after his longtime associate Kosygin. Abroad, Brezhnev's long reign will be most remembered for a decade of relaxed tensions in the world. At home, his tenure will ever endure as the era of Soviet stagnation. Brezhnev himself recognized the basic flaw in the Soviet Communist system and blamed the USSR's economic problems on the Council of Mutual Economic Assistance (Comecon), the Soviet Union's answer to the Marshall Plan. Shortly before his death, he told his comrades on the Politburo,

> The root of the problem lies in the fact that time has outgrown the forms that were created thirty years ago when the organization was founded. . . . Our economy is gigantic. Take any ministry—it's almost the size of an army. The government apparatus has proliferated. And we have far too many miscalculations and all kinds of misunderstandings.[42]

To cure the bureaucratic illnesses afflicting the failing Soviet economy, Brezhnez called for a tightening of discipline across the board, which served only to move the country closer to "the threshold of dramatic change."[43]

By the end of the Brezhnev era, the fatal flaw of communism had already infected the Soviet economy beyond any reasonable expectation of recovery. And to add to the woes of Brezhnev's successors, signals of growing national unrest were now being received in Moscow with alarming frequency.

Chapter 4 Soltet Dissent

The greatest villains of Shakespeare never went beyond ten or so cadavers, because they had no ideology. . . . It is thanks to ideology that the twentieth century has experienced villainy on a scale of millions. . . . Refuse to live according to the Lie.

—Aleksandr Solzhenitsyn

EAST-WEST TENSIONS relaxed during the 1970s, but the Soviets experienced troublesome upheavals at home. Two broad-based dissident movements emerged—one in defense of human rights, the other in resistance to government injustices against national minorities. Both movements shared a common cause against a totalitarian regime. Despite domestic repression and mixed feelings abroad in the decade of détente, both movements steadily gained strength. Two widely recognized Soviet human-rights activists were nuclear physicist Andrey Sakharov and author and essayist Aleksandr Solzhenitsyn.

A Painful Process

Aleksandr Solzhenitsyn achieved instant recognition in his homeland with the publication of his first book, *One Day in the Life of Ivan Denisovich,* in 1962. The short novel told the story of a single day in the life of an inmate of a Soviet labor camp. It was based on Solzhenitsyn's own experiences as a political prisoner. (A former artillery officer in World War II, Solzhenitsyn had been arrested in 1945 and served eight years in a labor camp—and three more years in exile in Kazakhstan—for having criticized Stalin in a private letter.) Solzhenitsyn's domestic acclaim did not last long. Following the publication of a collection of his short stories in 1963, the state banned further publication of his work, which it considered to be too critical of government repression.

Solzhenitsyn started circulating his works underground inside the Soviet Union and publishing them abroad. His later novels, *The First Circle* and *Cancer Ward*, both published abroad in 1968, dealt with his imprisonment and his hospitalization for cancer in Kazakhstan, respectively, and earned him the Nobel Prize for literature in 1970. He declined to travel to Stockholm to receive the prize, however, fearing that the Soviet Union would bar his readmittance upon his return. Solzhenitsyn's fears may well have been justified, for Yuri Andropov, the chairman of the KGB and later the successor to Leonid Brezhnev, was already exploring means to discredit Solzhenitsyn.

During the 1970s, activists such as Aleksandr Solzhenitsyn spoke out against the Soviet Union's totalitarian regime and human-rights violations.

After the Soviet suppression of democratic reforms in Czecho-slovakia in 1968, Andropov had set up the new KGB Fifth Direc-torate to monitor and crack down on all forms of dissent. He formed specialized departments within the directorate to scrutinize the activ-ities of students, intellectuals, nationalists from ethnic minorities, Jews, and other religious groups. Upon hearing the news of Solzhen-itsyn's selection for the Nobel Prize, Andropov immediately drafted a decree to the Politburo, hoping to strip the subversive author of his citizenship and expel him from the Soviet Union:

> When analyzing the materials on Solzhenitsyn and his works, one cannot fail to arrive at the conclusion that we are dealing with a political opponent of the Soviet state and social system. . . . If Solzhenitsyn continues to reside in the country after re-ceiving the Nobel Prize, it will strengthen his position, and al-low him to propagandize his views more actively.[44]

Andropov failed to persuade most Politburo members, who feared that Solzhenitsyn's ouster might invite adverse world opinion.

In the autumn of 1971, Interior Minister Nikolai Shchelokov suggested an alternative solution. "In this case what needs to be done is not to execute our enemies publicly but smother them with em-braces,"[45] he said. First Secretary Leonid Brezhnev agreed. But Shchelokov's proposed solution did not still the prolific pen of the Soviet Union's leading literary dissident.

In February 1974, shortly after the first volume of his monu-mental work *The Gulag Archipelago*—a history and memoir of life in the USSR's system of collective labor camps—was published in the West, KGB agents expelled Solzhenitsyn from the Soviet Union. Solzhenitsyn established residence first in Switzerland until 1976, and then in Cavendish, Vermont, where he continued to denounce Soviet oppression through his writings.

In 1994 Solzhenitsyn announced his intentions to return to Rus-sia, as he had always planned. When he arrived in Moscow on July 21, he told a crowd of well wishers and reporters, "Our country is collapsing. I never thought the exit from communism would be pain-less, but nobody would have thought it would be this painful."[46]

How much Solzhenitsyn contributed to the collapse of commu-nism in his homeland is impossible to quantify, but if a numeric value

Solzhenitsyn, flanked by his wife and sons, returns to Russia in 1994 after twenty years in exile.

could be placed on his contributions to the fall of Soviet communism, it would be a high number.

"A Figure of the Inner Spirit"

The written and oral word, though published in underground presses or spoken in whispers, spread truth across the farthest reaches of the vast Soviet Union during times of oppression and dissent. One flow of information emanated from the samizdat ("self-published," as opposed to *gozidat*, or "state-published") underground political publications that gained wide circulation in the late 1960s and 1970s. The samizdat, coupled with word of mouth, represented the chief mechanisms for spreading Soviet dissent and unrest. Nuclear physicist Andrey Sakharov, "the Father of the Soviet H-bomb," as he became known, used the samizdat to spread the word about human-rights injustices in the USSR.

Sakharov's threshold-crossing research in controlled thermonuclear fusion had led to the development of the Soviet Union's first hydrogen bomb. He was made a full member of the Academy of Sciences for his accomplishments. Starting in the late 1950s, though never a proponent of disarmament, he pioneered an effort to identify the dangers of radioactive fallout and pushed for a cessation of nuclear testing. Soviet officials initially scorned his efforts but later credited him with helping to bring about the Nuclear Test Ban Treaty of 1963, which was signed by the United States, Great Britain, and the Soviet Union on August 5 of that year.

Moving on from these political activities, Sakharov started expressing his concern about a range of scientific and global issues. He warned of environmental pollution and advocated Soviet-American cooperation. Sakharov achieved universal prominence when his ten-thousand-word essay "Progress, Coexistence, and Intellectual Freedom," which had circulated as a samizdat manifesto, was republished in the *New York Times.*

In the essay Sakharov declared that "the exposure of Stalin [de-Stalinization] must be carried through to the end." He characterized Stalinism as resembling fascism but exhibiting "a much more subtle kind of hypocrisy and demagogy [appeal to human emotions or prejudices rather than to reason]. It relied "not on an openly cannibalistic program like Hitler's but on a progressive, scientific, and popular socialist ideology [that] served as a convenient screen for deceiving the working class"[47] and causing other evils.

Sakharov opposed the power monopoly of the Communist Party and spoke out strongly for human rights, intellectual freedom, and the rule of law. While many of Sakharov's peers doubted the ability of the Soviet masses to govern themselves, he believed that only freedom, under the guidance of the intellectuals, would "squeeze the slave out of the Russian people."[48]

During the 1970s Sakharov argued that Soviet industry had reached a dead end from which only greater freedom of the people could provide an escape. His passionate defense of human rights earned him the Nobel Peace Prize in 1975. But his continuing aspersions against the neo-Stalinists, or new, latter-day advocates of Stalinism, did not endear him to the Brezhnev regime.

Sakharov's brusque criticism of the USSR's invasion of Afghanistan in 1979 finally grew intolerable to Brezhnev. "There is a limit to everything," Brezhnev declared. "To leave his attacks without a response is impossible."[49] Brezhnev exiled his critic to the closed city of Gorki (modern-day Nizhniy Novgorod) in central European Russia. Sakharov remained there, with his access to the West denied, until recalled to Moscow by Mikhail Gorbachev in 1986. Sakharov's recall represented a signal to the world from the new Soviet leader that a new age had dawned in the Soviet Union.

Back in Moscow, Sakharov found it difficult to regain his political voice. When Soviet historian Mikhail Gefter inquired about his health, Sakharov replied sadly, "It is difficult to live now. People write me, they visit, and they are all hoping that I will be able to help somehow. But I am powerless."[50] Sakharov underestimated his power to lead and inspire his countrymen. In the late 1980s Tatyana Zaslavskaya, a leading sociologist whose vision helped to fashion the early Soviet reforms, said this of Sakharov:

> Sakharov was the only one among us who made no compromises. For us, he was a figure of the inner spirit. Just the bare facts of his life, the way he suffered for us all, gave him authority that no one else had. Without him, we could not begin to rebuild our society or our selves.[51]

Nobel Peace Prize recipient Andrey Sakharov appears with his wife in this photograph taken while in exile in Gorki.

Beginning of the End

Challenges to Communist rule in the Eastern European satellites compounded domestic crises arising from ethnic nationalism in the late 1980s. In 1989 the so-called Brezhnev Doctrine was tested and defeated in Poland, Hungary, Czechoslovakia, and East Germany.

Solidarity, the Polish independent trade union headed by Lech Walesa, who had been all but extinguished by the Soviet-backed military dictator General Wojciech Jaruzelski, suddenly sprang back to life. In June 1989, in the first free elections since the establishment of the Eastern bloc, Solidarity's anti-Communist candidates' landslide victories, signaling the beginning of the end of Communist rule.

Hungary followed. In October 1989 the Hungarian Socialist Workers' (Communist) Party voted itself out of existence and a new democratic era began.

In December 1989, during the "Velvet Revolution" in Czechoslovakia, large-scale demonstrations spawned the resignation of the Communist-dominated cabinet. The first government in forty-one years without a Communist majority succeeded it. The revolt's association with velvet derives from the ease in which the change occurred.

In *The Rise and Fall of the Soviet Empire,* Brian Crozier quotes a December 4 statement from Moscow officially condemning the Soviet occupation of Czechoslovakia as "an interference in the internal affairs of sovereign Czechoslovakia." Moscow's statement marked the end of the Brezhnev Doctrine.

Little more than ten months later, foreign ministers of West Germany, East Germany, the United States, Great Britain, France, and the Soviet Union met in Moscow to sign a treaty on the final settlement of Germany: the reunification of the Federal Republic of (West) Germany and the (East) German Democratic Republic. This event amounted to a formal end to the Cold War—and heralded the beginning of the end of the Soviet empire.

Andrey Sakharov did not live to see the breakup of the Soviet Union. He died quietly in Moscow on December 14, 1989, only nine months after his election to the new Soviet legislature. Hundreds of thousands of Sakharov's admirers attended his funeral. As they filed past his grave, many of them dropped notes saying, "Forgive us."[52] Saints and martyrs and defenders of human rights could scarcely ask for a more fitting epitaph.

Soviet dissidents such as Solzhenitsyn and Sakharov probably never numbered more than three thousand. They were mostly intellectuals. Despite their small numbers, their impact on Soviet society—particularly on the Soviet leadership—was astonishing. Their stands for human rights and against totalitarian abuses contributed greatly to the opening of Soviet society in the mid-1980s—which would, in turn, hasten the demise of Soviet communism.

The Rise of Ethnic Nationalism

By the mid-1970s human-rights dissidence began tapering off, with help from the Helsinki Final Act (Helsinki Accords) of 1975. In addition to an East-West agreement on the postwar national boundaries of Eastern European countries, the act invoked a Soviet agreement to respect and protect the human rights of people in these regions. Although the act failed to provide any enforcement mechanisms, some observers feel that it began the dismantling of the Soviet empire in Eastern Europe. Equally significant was the rise of ethnic nationalism among Soviet minorities and satellite states.

From Lenin's time to Gorbachev's, the most puzzling and enduring problem faced by Soviet rulers was the nationalities issue. More than one hundred nationalities resided within the vast confines of the USSR. The Soviet Union was split into near-equal divisions of

Hundreds of thousands of mourners attended the funeral of Sakharov, who had become a hero to human-rights activists throughout the Soviet Union.

The Union of Soviet Socialist Republics

In the tumultuous wake of the 1917 Bolshevik Revolution in Russia, four socialist republics were established in the territories once ruled by the czars: the Russian and Transcaucasian Soviet Federated Republics and the Ukrainian and Byelorussian Soviet Socialist Republics. On December 30, 1922, these four republics united to form the Union of Soviet Socialist Republics (the Soviet Union or USSR). The Soviet Union, with Moscow as its capital, thereafter formally succeeded the Russian empire on July 6, 1923, and became the first state based on Marxist socialism (communism).

In the years that followed, additional republics joined the union. The Transcaucasian Republic was abolished in 1936 and its territory redistributed to establish three new Soviet socialist republics (SSRs): Armenia, Azerbaijan, and Georgia. From 1940 to 1991, the Soviet Union consisted of these three SSRs and twelve others: Byelorussia (Belarus), Estonia, Kazakhstan, Kyrgyzstan (Kirghizia), Latvia, Lithuania, Moldavia (Moldova), Russia, Tajikistan (Tadzhikistan), Turkmenistan, Ukraine, and Uzbekistan. It also contained twenty autonomous, or self-governing, SSRs—sixteen within Russia, two within Georgia, and one each within Azerbaijan and Uzbekistan.

From the time of its establishment in 1922 until its breakup in 1991, the Soviet Union was, by area, the largest nation in the world, covering some 8,650,000 square miles and occupying one-sixth of the earth's land mass. Seven times the area of India and two and one-half times the size of the United States, its lateral boundaries stretched more than 6,800 miles—from the Baltic Sea in the west to the Bering Strait in the east—and included eleven of the world's twenty-four time zones. Its northern limits bordered on the Arctic Ocean, and its southern extremities extended some 2,800 miles southward to Afghanistan.

some 145 million ethnic Russians and about 140.6 million non-Russians. Commencing with the Khrushchev regime, Communist Party elites in the non-Russian republics, which had become entrenched as regional power centers by then, often displayed remarkable resistance to the dictates of the central power structure in Moscow.

As the economy began to crumble under the weight of the arms, space, and technology races, and from the ongoing demands of Soviet expansionism in Europe and Asia as well as abroad, the rise of ethnic nationalism began to plague Moscow with four distinct kinds of ethnic problems: first, ethnic conflicts between the majority and minority ethnic groups in the republics; second, resistance of non-Russian national movements to the traditional rule by the Soviet center; third, the "Russian question" or Russian nationalism; and fourth, the growing numbers of displaced persons, either living outside of their homeland or with no territory designated for them.

The first problem in this polyglot nation of 15 union republics, 20 autonomous republics, and a miscellany of 138 additional provinces, districts, and regions involved ethnic conflicts between majority and minority nationalities in the 15 union republics. One of the early indications of trouble occurred in December 1986, twenty-one months after Mikhail Gorbachev took office as the last general secretary of the Soviet Union.

Gorbachev, in a seeming lapse of sensitivity, replaced Din-mukhamed Kunaev, Communist Party chief in Kazakhstan and an ethnic Kazakh, with Gennady V. Kolbin, an ethnic Russian. Kunaev's replacement fomented violent conflicts in Kazakhstan and provoked mass demonstrations in the streets of its capital, Alma-Ata, and in other cities in Kazakhstan. In time, Gorbachev realized his mistake:

> Only later did I understand that this was not the way to proceed, that we could not live by a double standard—[calling for democracy, while imposing solutions "decisively."] . . . But what had happened made me think seriously about the nationalities questions.[53]

In February 1988 Armenians in the mountainous enclave of Karabakh, Azerbaijan, gave Gorbachev more to think about when they began demonstrating for a merger with the adjacent republic of Armenia. Not unexpectedly, the Azerbaijanis protested. "In Karabakh, matters moved very quickly to the point of direct clashes between representatives of the two different national communities," Gorbachev wrote after leaving office, "and a short time later to outright war between those communities and between the Armenian and Azerbaijan republics."[54]

Similar conflicts occurred in Georgia when the Abghaz and Osetin nationalities protested Georgian attempts to reduce their control over their autonomous republics. In Moldavia, the Turkic Gagauc people and the Slavic people revolted against a growing pro-Romanian movement among the Moldavian majority. (Moldavia had once belonged to Romania, but was lost to the Soviet Union after World War II because of Romania's affiliation with Nazi Germany.) And in Central Asia, the Uzbeks drove out the Meskhetian Turks, fellow Muslims who had been exiled there by Stalin from his home republic of Georgia. Trouble flared all across the southern areas in the summer of 1989.

By the end of the year, the Baltic republics of Estonia, Latvia, and Lithuania in the north dramatically illustrated the second kind of ethnic problem then facing Gorbachev and the Moscow power structure. Seeking democratic reform and self-determination, the three nations (all of which had been annexed by the Soviet Union in 1940) openly revolted. The separatist movement grew faster and more radically in the Baltic republics and in Caucasia (Georgia, Armenia, Azerbaijan, who had joined the USSR in 1936, and part of southern Russia in Europe) than anywhere else in the Soviet Union.

Meanwhile, increasingly during the decade of the 1980s, the "Russian question" posed a third kind of ethnic problem. The Russian Soviet Federated Soviet Republic (RSFSR), unlike its fellow

Lithuanians rally together to demand democratic reform in 1989.

republics, was not independently functional apart from the Soviet Union. Many of its institutions were merged with all-Soviet institutions. With the winds of change now swirling across the land, Russian nationalists such as Boris Yeltsin saw a new role for the Russian federation and began demanding Russian rights. Yeltsin, arguing that the RSFSR had become the ultimate victim of Soviet imperialism, said, "The issue of primary importance is the spiritual, national, and economic rebirth of Russia, which has been for long decades an appendage of the center and which in many respects has lost its independence."[55] Millions of Russians were listening approvingly to a voice that would soon change the fabric of their lives. In sum, citizens of the Russian republic wanted the same rights, privileges, and independence from all-Soviet institutions that the rest of the Soviet republics already enjoyed.

At the same time, the fourth ethnic problem was making itself felt in diasporas (colonies of displaced or otherwise relocated peoples) within the Soviet Union. These were people who either had migrated outside their ethnic homeland or had no specified area to call home. They numbered some 60 million in 1989, almost half of them Russian. Great numbers of Ukrainians, Tatars, Armenians, and Jews made up most of the migrant or stateless remainder. As the trend toward ethnically distinct nation-states grew, the Russians and other diaspora peoples feared that they would become exiles in their own former country. Their fears fomented dissent and demands for equal status and rights. These colonies provided the largest support base favoring the continuation of some kind of federated multinational state.

The central Soviet government had held these forces of disparate interests in check for several decades, but as the Soviets moved toward democratization, ethnic demands and dissent increased alarmingly, accelerating the breakup of the USSR. "As the center grew weaker, nationalist movements escalated from cultural and linguistic demands to calls for sovereignty and independence," writes Ronald Grigor Suny, professor of political science at the University of Chicago. "Thus, the empire's disintegration began in Moscow and was initiated from the top."[56] The chief instruments of the final phase of its disintegration were the twin policies of glasnost and perestroika, both of which were initiated and implemented by Mikhail Gorbachev.

Glasnost and
Chapter 5 Perestroika

*I am convinced that a necessary stage on humanity's path to-
ward a new state of being must be, and cannot help but be,
a renewal of its thinking.*
　　　　　　—Mikhail S. Gorbachev, last general secretary
　　　　　　　　　　and president of the Soviet Union

AT ABOUT 6:00 P.M. on Christmas Day 1991, Mikhail Gorbachev arrived at his office on the third floor of the Kremlin, in Moscow, adjacent to the Politburo conference hall.
Several of his aides joined him there, assuming that the last leader of
the Soviet Union did not want to be left alone with the nuclear but-
ton while he drafted his letter of resignation.

A few minutes before 7:00 P.M., Gorbachev proceeded to an ante-
room where a makeshift television studio had been set up for a telecast
that would reach some 153 nations around the world. Borrowing a pen
from a CNN broadcast executive, Gorbachev sat at a desk and signed
his just-completed resignation statement. At precisely 7:00 P.M., he
faced the television cameras and began reading from a prepared text.

One last time, Gorbachev tried to explain to the Soviet people
and to the world why he had initiated perestroika in the first place.
Despite an abundance of land, oil, and other natural resources, he
told his audience, the Soviet Union had been lagging behind Western
countries. He voiced his pride over his role in ending the Cold War
and in aiding Soviet citizens to regain their freedom. As he neared
the end of his ten-minute address, he emphasized a few sentences
that he had hastily inserted at the last minute:

It is vitally important to preserve the democratic achievements of the last few years. They have been paid for through the suffering of our entire history, our tragic experience. They must not be given up, under any circumstances or under any pretext. Otherwise all our hopes for a better future will be dashed.[57]

At 7:35 P.M., less than a half hour after Gorbachev finished his address, the red hammer-and-sickle flag of the USSR was lowered from the Kremlin for the last time.

Gorbachev's Compass

Mikhail Sergeyevich Gorbachev, the first Soviet leader to be born after the creation of the Soviet Union, had set out to save communism and fashion a better life for his people through the twin policies of perestroika (restructuring) and glasnost (openness). His goals were utopian; his task, all but impossible. In the end, the march of history trampled roughshod over his idealistic aims and left him, his party, and his nation behind to molder in the dust of broken dreams and dismembered empires.

Gorbachev and Yeltsin touch hands before giving a parliament speech in 1991. Two months after this photograph was taken, Gorbachev resigned from office.

Gorbachev, born to a peasant family near Stavropol in the North Caucasus in 1931, began studying law at Moscow State University and joined the Communist Party in 1952. At the university he met Raisa Titorenko, a young woman from a small town in Siberia. He married her in 1953. After graduating in 1955, Mikhail and Raisa returned to his home region, where he began a steady rise in party organizations, leading to his election as first secretary of the regional committee in Stavropol in 1970. The following year he won election to the party's Central Committee.

In 1978 Gorbachev was appointed secretary for agriculture, a position that brought him to Moscow. Two years later he was made a full member of the Politburo. He further enhanced his place in the Soviet scheme of things, singing the praises of Leonid Brezhnev. He spoke glowingly of the doddering Soviet leader's "titanic daily work" that was "raising the well-being of workers and strengthening the peace and security of nations."[58]

Building Bridges

Shortly after winning election as Soviet general secretary, Mikhail Gorbachev received a visit from Thomas "Tip" O'Neill, Speaker of the U.S. House of Representatives, on April 10, 1985. In *Gorbachev: On My Country and the World*, Gorbachev discusses the concerns that he shared with O'Neill over the freeze in Soviet-American relations:

> The relations between our countries are presently in a kind of ice age. We favor restoring Soviet-American relations to normal channels. At bottom, our position includes the understanding that *a fatal conflict of interest between our countries is not inevitable.* Further, we have a common interest—in avoiding nuclear war, in guaranteeing the security of both our countries, of preserving life itself for our respective peoples. . . . We do not wish to remake the United States in our own image, regardless of what we like or dislike about that nation. However, the United States should not undertake the quixotic [foolishly idealistic] task of remaking the Soviet Union to suit its own tastes. That would just lead to war. . . . Many problems exist in the world—political, economic, social—but there is a way out, namely, peaceful coexistence, *the recognition that each nation has the right to live as it wishes. There is no other alternative.* . . . We must build a bridge toward cooperation. But to build such a bridge, as everyone knows, construction must proceed from both sides.

Following Brezhnev's death in 1982 and the deaths of his successors, Yuri Andropov and Konstantin Chernenko, within another twenty-
eight months, Gorbachev easily won election as general secretary on
March 11, 1985. At his first plenum, or general assembly, on April 23,
he declared his political philosophy and vowed to uphold it:

> The whole of life and the entire course of history confirms
> convincingly the great truth of Leninist teaching. It has been
> and it remains for us a guide to action, a source of inspira-
> tion, a true compass for fixing the strategy and tactics of our
> movement forward.[59]

At age fifty-three, the peasant's son from Stavropol now stood at
the helm of the Soviet ship of state—a ship that had drifted off
course. Using seventy-year-old Leninist doctrine and methods for a
compass, Gorbachev intended to shape a new course for Soviet communism.

Gorbachev's Gamble

Although Gorbachev was an accomplished politician, his policy of perestroika smashed a hole in the prow of the Soviet ship. The ship began
taking on water immediately and within five years it slipped beneath the
waves of glasnost. Gorbachev had taken the helm in a sea of stagnation
left behind by the eighteen-year-long reign of Leonid Brezhnev. He believed that the course out of the Brezhnev doldrums lay in returning the
USSR to its Leninist origins. He intended not to eliminate communism
but rather to revitalize it and improve its efficiency through reforms and
restructuring (perestroika), openness and publicity (glasnost), and democratization (*demokratizatsiia*). Gorbachev meant for perestroika to
reshape not only the party structure but also all of the institutions of the
Soviet society and economy. Soviet institutions had grown too large for
too long, resulting in duplicated functions and overlapping jurisdic-
tions. A thorough housecleaning and streamlining was needed to eliminate inefficiency and waste.

Glasnost would expose the abuses of the existing system to public scrutiny, generate new ideas, and help to eliminate obstacles in the
path of improvements. *Demokratizatsiia*—that is, a closely regulated
form of public participation—would tap the energy of the masses and
animate the reformation process. Gorbachev explains:

Without the citizens' understanding and support, without their participation, it would not have been possible to move from dead center. That is why we initiated the policies of perestroika and glasnost simultaneously.

Like perestroika itself, glasnost made its way with considerable difficulty. The nomenklatura [members of the party apparatus] on all levels, which regarded the strictest secrecy and protection of authorities from criticism from below as the holy of holies of the regime, opposed glasnost in every way they could, both openly and secretly, trampling its first shoots in the local press. Even among the most sincere supporters of perestroika, the tradition over many years of making everything a secret made itself felt. But it was precisely glasnost that awakened people from their social slumber, helped them overcome indifference and passivity and become aware of the stake they had in change and of its important implications for their lives. . . . In short, without glasnost there would have been no perestroika.[60]

Gorbachev gambled that by informing the people of the true state of their society and its economy, he would win their support for his reforms. He totally misread how the people would react to his reopening of the heretofore closed Soviet society. His gamble turned into a miscalculation on the grandest scale.

A Glimpse of Glasnost

Glasnost went well at first, as the Soviet citizenry basked in the light of revelation in their new, open society. But the winds of change soon blew up a storm as the people learned more about their government and what it had been up to for more than six decades. "As soon as the public began to learn the truth about the regime and its countless myths, the foundations of the system began to crack," writes Dmitri Volkogonov. "Truth was a weapon against which the Leninist system was now [under Gorbachev] powerless to fight."[61] The people openly criticized Marxism-Leninism, Stalinism, communism, the Soviet intervention in Afghanistan, a failing economy that provided less than even a dreary existence, and the ongoing governmental litany of unfulfilled promises for still more openness. Not even Gorbachev escaped criticism.

During a 1988 television appearance, Vitaly Korotich, editor of the Soviet magazine *Ogonyok*, echoed the people's frustration over glasnost. He viewed glasnost, or freedom of expression, as a basic human right and not as the great privilege or feat that Gorbachev and his minions made it out to be:

> For me, glasnost is simply a return to the norm, nothing special. We have already started saying it's some feat to print [Boris] Pasternak [author of the novel *Doctor Zhivago*], a feat to print [the great poet Anna] Akhmatova. But what the hell kind of feat is this? The hero [Khrushchev] is the one who banned them, and what we are doing is a normal act. They still try to convince us that if we speak the truth a lot, then something will come crashing down in our country. I will be terribly glad if everything that collapses because of the truth collapses immediately.[62]

In 1988 the gap was already widening between how the Communists defined reform and how the people perceived its application. While Gorbachev was battling to stave off the collapse of communism, Korotich was looking forward to it.

Taking advantage of freedom of expression under Gorbachev's leadership, a homeless man protests government policy in 1989.

Glasnost Slays the Giant

Many forces acted together to topple Soviet communism. Perhaps none was more important than glasnost. In *Dismantling Utopia*, Scott Shane, a former Moscow correspondent for the *Baltimore Sun*, makes the case for "openness."

> Gorbachev had designed glasnost, this old Russian notion of the public airing of problems, as a blowtorch that could strip layers of old and peeling paint from Soviet society. But the Communist system proved dry tinder. From the first touch of flame the conservatives began to warn that glasnost was in danger of igniting the entire edifice of Soviet Communism. Gorbachev meanwhile was insisting, "No, no, don't worry, comrades, we're just going to renovate the place, everything's fine." Later, as the conflagration began . . . Gorbachev seemed unwilling to accept the consequences of the reforms he had initiated. . . . In his vacillation, he confirmed that his original intentions were more modest than his Western admirers sometimes imputed to him. He had come to save the system, not to bury it.
>
> Mikhail Gorbachev, a giant and fascinating figure, has had numerous chroniclers and will justifiably have many more. But by focusing on the dynamism and boldness of Gorbachev and the unprecedented drama of Kremlin politics in the late 1980s, Western writers have underplayed certain bigger, impersonal forces that drove a superpower into reform, then revolution, and finally collapse.
>
> The most important of these forces was information. Information is the most revealing prism through which to view the essence and the end of the Soviet Union. Information slew the totalitarian giant.

Paradoxes

Gorbachev reached the zenith of his reform process in the spring and early summer of 1988, presiding over three major events. The first key event was the one thousandth anniversary of the founding of the Orthodox Church in Russia in 988. By observing its birth, the state at last extended an olive branch to the church and formally recognized the religion it had for so long persecuted. God had finally returned to the Soviet Union.

The second significant event was U.S. president Ronald Reagan's visit to Moscow for a summit meeting with his Soviet counterpart. Reagan addressed the students of Moscow University on May 31, enthralling them with glowing predictions of the bright futures that lay ahead for all in a new Soviet Union of free thought and speech. They gave him "a standing ovation that [beat] against Lenin's carved colossus [bust] like waves of an imminent storm."[63] Fresh hopes for friendlier East-West relations resonated in every hand clap.

The third notable event was the Nineteenth Conference of the Communist Party of the Soviet Union that convened on June 28. During the conference, Gorbachev established political liberalization—for example, permitting more than one political party—and orchestrated the party's acceptance of non-Communist organizations. The West now found cause to applaud, as the Soviets moved toward democratization.

By then, Gorbachev's "new thinking"—particularly his efforts toward lessening world tensions in the spirit of international cooperation—had endeared him to the West. His popularity in the West, often called "Gorbymania," had begun in 1984. During a trip to England, his first visit to the West, he charmed British prime minister Margaret Thatcher into commenting that here at last was "a Communist I can do business with."[64]

Gorbachev's efforts at reform made him popular with Westerners. British prime minister Margaret Thatcher (right) was one of his many admirers.

Gorbachev's popularity rose higher in 1985, when he started presenting arms-reduction proposals during a visit to France, which ultimately led to the U.S.-Soviet agreement to reduce intermediate-range nuclear forces (INF Treaty), which was signed by Reagan and Gorbachev in 1987. Beyond question, a defense budget consuming more than 20 percent of the Soviet gross national product added to Gorbachev's motivation for arms reduction.

(Some authorities on Soviet defense spending estimate that it totaled far more than 20 percent. As a case in point, Dmitri Volkogonov, former adviser to Boris Yeltsin, claims, "Seventy percent of the state budget was being spent on military needs [in 1983], although this figure was never disclosed."[65] Whatever the numbers, it was clearly in Gorbachev's best interest to seek means of reducing arms and thereby the defense spending that held the Soviet economy in a death grip.)

Gorbachev, the consummate politician and manipulator, relied heavily on his popularity abroad to grease the skids for launching his political, economic, and social reforms at home. Paradoxically, however, the more he reformed the system, the more unstable it became. The more he convinced the West of a new Soviet attitude toward its Eastern European satellites, the less able he was to control events within them. His every forward step toward reforms of any kind was nullified by an intransigent bureaucracy intent on preserving the status quo and a privileged place in the party power structure. The more the world came to love him, the more glasnost's open society came to abhor him.

Perhaps the greatest paradoxes of all resided in the man himself: Gorbachev refused to concede that Soviet communism did not work and clung to its Leninist doctrines; he championed democratization but disdained democracy and never granted free elections; he aspired to the presidency of the Soviet Union but achieved the office only by manipulation, refusing to face a public electorate; he flirted with a free market but ultimately rejected it; he promised agricultural reforms but refused to decollectivize the farm system or to desubsidize farm prices; he promised landownership rights, then delayed legalizing private property; and he encouraged the republics to voice their demands, then refused to grant them. Such were the paradoxes of Gorbachev and his methods, which led inevitably to his fall.

Mikhail and Boris

Soviet president Mikhail Gorbachev experienced a blustery relationship at best with his political rival Boris Yeltsin, president of the Russian Federation. In an interview recorded in *Lenin's Tomb*, David Remnick, a former Moscow correspondent for the *Washington Post*, asked Gorbachev if he kept in contact with Yeltsin. The following is Gorbachev's reply.

> He never calls me. I called him several times at first, but from his side there has never been a call. Boris Nikolayevich knows everything! We have no relations. What kind of personal relations can there be when his press secretary publishes a statement saying that they will take measures against Gorbachev, that they will put him in his place? What relations can there be? This is ruled out.
>
> The democrats [Yeltsin's party] have failed to use their power. Look how much they struggled for power and how much they promised. There were even statements that the Russian president would lay himself down across the railroad tracks if living standards went down. Well, now they've gone down fifty percent! The tracks must be occupied.
>
> They have to tell the people how they are going to get through the winter, what there will be to eat, whether there will be any heat, and what will happen to reforms. And they have no answer. They don't know what to say. They need to play for time and they need to find a lightning rod. It's amazing—Yeltsin's team, the Constitutional Court, and the fundamentalists who defended against the August coup are all in this struggle together against Gorbachev. This is phenomenal!

Collision Course

On June 12, 1987, U.S. president Ronald Reagan stood before the Brandenburg Gate of the infamous Berlin Wall—the concrete wall separating East and West Berlin that had been erected at Nikita Khrushchev's direction in 1961. In a dramatic event staged for television, Reagan declaimed, "Mr. Gorbachev, tear down this wall!"[66]

While visiting West Germany two years later, Soviet general secretary Mikhail Gorbachev spoke of that same wall on June 15 and declared that "nothing is eternal in this world."[67] The wall was breached on the following November 9, and souvenir hunters began breaking it apart with pickaxes and sledgehammers. It was not eternal—no more than was the short, unhappy reign of the last Soviet ruler. The Cold War was fading into history—and Gorbachev's decline had begun.

Gorbachev's popularity crested in the West at year's end. As the world ushered in the year 1990, a *Time* magazine editorial portrayed him as "the Copernicus, Darwin and Freud of Communism all wrapped in one."[68] The newsmagazine named him Man of the Decade. But at home, the best-selling weekly *Argumenti i Fakti* noted that Gorbachev had not reached the top ten in popularity.

While Soviet troops withdrew from Eastern bloc nations that had opted for freedom and democracy over communism, and Soviet republics were demanding their independence in bloody displays of violence all across Europe and Asia, the Soviet state split into two factions: those who wanted to preserve communism and those who wanted to abolish it. Boris Yeltsin, who was soon to become president of the new Russian republic, defined himself as a popularist and flatly declared that those who remained Communists were fantasists. Gorbachev responded sharply: "I am a Communist, a convinced Communist. For some that may be a fantasy. But for me it is my own goal."[69]

The fall of the Berlin Wall in 1989 was one of the events that signaled the collapse of the Soviet Union and accelerated the end of the Cold War.

While starvation and hardship was the norm for Soviet citizens in the early 1990s, rumors flew that Gorbachev's wife, Raisa (right), was living an extravagant lifestyle.

In his actions, however, Gorbachev succumbed to a political ambivalence that undermined his ability to govern and control his constituents. He welcomed the new freedoms in the former satellite countries but denied the demands of the Baltic nations for self-determination. As factions on the ultra right and liberal left polarized, Gorbachev tried to preserve communism while encouraging greater freedom and democratization. In his efforts to please both sides, he succeeded only in aggravating all interests at every level.

Meanwhile, rumors of impending starvation reached the West with growing regularity as the Soviets dumped gold and diamonds on declining world markets to buy food. Bloodshed in the republics, rail and mining strikes, long lines for food and living essentials, poor harvests, increased prices, and dwindling supplies became the norm in the Soviet Union while Soviet citizens exchanged rumors of Raisa Gorbachev's exorbitant lifestyle. Yet Western eyes continued to view Gorbachev as a new-age St. George, the slayer of the Communist dragon. But at what cost?

Alexander Bukhanov, the influential and discontented editor of *Sovyetskaya Literatura*, noted that Gorbachev had destroyed everything we believed in, everything that kept us together. Gorbachev hasn't built anything new, he hasn't thrown us a lifebelt [life preserver]! Everyone, me included, is on a sinking ship, on a plane that is crashing, and that's what terrifies us.[70]

Boris Yeltsin sensed a similar loss of direction and control. "Our ship has lost its anchor," he conceded to visiting U.S. congressional leaders. "So we are all feeling a little sick."[71] The rocks of revolt now loomed dead ahead of the Soviet ship of state—and its pilot was running fast on a collision course.

The Coup

The inevitable shipwreck of the Soviet system came in 1991, far sooner and with far greater suddenness than most of the world could begin to imagine. From January 2 through 13, increasing Soviet intervention in Lithuania culminated in a bloody battle at a television tower in Vilnius, the nation's capital. Soviet Ministry of Internal Affairs, or secret police, troops opened fire on crowds of protesters,

Soviets struggle to buy sausages at a state-run market. Waiting in long lines and paying exorbitant prices became common for most Soviets during Gorbachev's term.

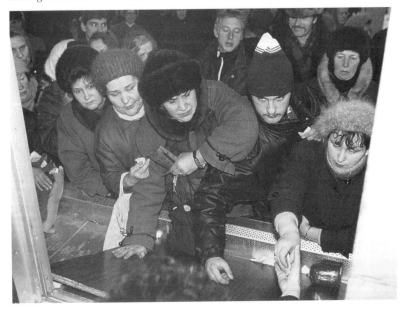

killing fourteen and wounding hundreds of others. Perestroika gave way to *perestrelka* (a shoot-out). In a speech on January 22, Gorbachev said,

> The events that occurred in Vilnius are in no way an expression of the policy of the president; it was not for this that presidential power was established. I therefore reject all speculation, all suspicions, and all insinuations in this regard.[72]

In other words, Gorbachev denied having ordered the carnage in Vilnius. But the people did not believe him. The *Moscow News* printed a front-page editorial decrying the "death throes" of the regime that had executed a "criminal act" in Lithuania: "After the bloody Sunday in Vilnius, what is left of our president's favorite topics of 'humane socialism,' 'new thinking,' and a 'common European home'? Virtually nothing."[73] The deck boards of the Soviet ship had begun to shudder and shake under the widespread feet of Gorbachev as he struggled to maintain equilibrium. Events threatening the continuance of his regime moved swiftly now.

On March 17 Gorbachev, seeking to save the Union, put forth a referendum on the question "Do you consider necessary the preservation of the Union of Soviet Socialist Republics as a renewed federation of equal sovereign republics, in which the rights and freedom of an individual of any nationality will be fully guaranteed?"[74] With 80 percent of the electorate voting, 76.4 percent came out for the Soviet Union.

Two weeks later, the Warsaw Pact alliance dissolved in a sea of change, further evidence of which was demonstrated on June 12, when Boris Yeltsin was swept into the presidency of the new Russian Federation (still part of the USSR) by an overwhelming popular vote. Six weeks later Gorbachev stood tall in the eyes of the Western world one last time, when he joined U.S. president George Bush in signing the Strategic Arms Reduction Treaty (START) in the Kremlin on July 31. Then came the crash.

On August 19, 1991, hard-line extremists of Gorbachev's regime staged a coup—a sudden attempt to seize power—while Gorbachev and his wife were vacationing in the Crimea. Calling themselves the State Committee for the State of Emergency in the USSR, the extremists held the president and his spouse under house arrest in their quarters while they attempted to establish a temporary regime allegedly devoted to national unity and restoration. But their ill-planned and -executed coup attempt interfered with the signing of the New Union Treaty (through which Gorbachev had hoped to preserve the Soviet Union) that had been scheduled for August 22. The disintegration of the Soviet Union began on August 25, when Byelorussia declared its independence, and the treaty was never signed.

On the same day, while standing on a tank outside the White House in Moscow, Russian president Boris Yeltsin roared defiance at the coup-makers and declared their new government illegal. "You can build a throne of bayonets," he taunted the conspirators, "but you cannot sit on it for long."[75] His courage was perhaps the single most decisive factor in thwarting the coup.

The Voyage Ends

Gorbachev returned to Moscow on August 22. Amid the chaos of his floundering government, he resigned as general secretary of the discredited Communist Party of the Soviet Union three days later. Less than three months after Gorbachev's resignation as general secretary,

Yeltsin addresses a crowd during the coup attempt by hard-line extremists, declaring the conspirators' government illegal.

on November 6, President Yeltsin abolished the Communist Party in Russia and confiscated all of its property.

When voters in Ukraine chose independence from the Soviet Union on December 1, the end drew near for Gorbachev. Two days later, he called for the maintenance of the USSR. But Yeltsin hastened Gorbachev's free fall from the heights of power by recognizing Ukraine as an independent state. On December 8, Russia, Ukraine, and Belarus signed an agreement creating the Commonwealth of Independent States (CIS) as the successor to the Soviet Union. Mikhail Gorbachev resigned as president of the Soviet Union on December 25, 1991.

Perestroika had failed him; the truth of glasnost had prevailed in the end. After a tempestuous sixty-nine-year voyage, the Soviet ship of state had finally slipped beneath the sea.

Shortly after the red hammer-and-sickle flag of the Soviet Union was hauled down from the Kremlin for the last time, the white, red, and blue tricolor of Boris Yeltsin's Russia rose in its place. A small gathering of onlooking tourists in Red Square clapped or whistled their approval in the hush of a light-falling snow.

A War Without Winners

Epilogue

There were some of us to whom it was quite clear . . . that the Soviet regime as we had known it was not there for all time. We could not know when or how it would be changed. We knew only that the change was inevitable and impending.

— George F. Kennan, U.S. ambassador
to the Soviet Union in 1952

THE SOVIET UNION COLLAPSED soon after it lost control of its satellite nations. It lost control of its satellites because it could no longer afford the high cost of propping up the Marxist governments of the Eastern bloc nations. It could no longer support the expansionist aims of communism in Europe and around the world when it could no longer feed its people at home. The day inevitably came when the people went to the cupboard and found it bare. When they turned to their leaders for help, their leaders reached into the state coffers for more rubles and found the till empty. The fatal flaw of communism had caught up with the big spenders in the top-heavy Soviet bureaucracy. And the Soviet Union died not by the sword of a Cold War antagonist but from long years of economic mismanagement, corruption, and waste.

On Christmas Day 1991, U.S. president George Bush, in an address to the American public, lauded Mikhail Gorbachev "for his intellect, vision, and courage" and credited him with ending the Cold War. The president also said that the demise of the Soviet Union was a "victory for democracy and freedom."[76] Although President Bush

84

President Bush credited Gorbachev for ending the Cold War and praised him for his courage and vision.

and many others in the West were quick to claim victory in the Cold War, in the end it was a war without winners.

War Is No Option

Clearly, the collapse of Soviet communism and the breakup of the Soviet Union stand unchallenged as the most dramatic and visible results of the Cold War. The doctrine of Karl Marx and Friedrich Engels proved not only unworkable but finally unwanted in practice; the world's first socialist nation fell victim to a flawed economy incapable of sustaining an arms race, an expansionist empire, or even itself. Not even glasnost and perestroika could save a system already beyond rescue; openness and restructuring served only to hasten its demise. A discredited doctrine, a fallen nation, and a lost empire must surely invalidate any Soviet claim to victory in the Cold War.

Likewise, the high price paid by the Western powers for waging the Cold War—particularly the costs incurred by the United States—impugns the wisdom of naming either side the victor in this fifty-year war of nerves and the continuing threat of nuclear extinction. Hot wars in Korea and Vietnam, which originated largely because of the

Cold War, claimed the lives of nearly one hundred thousand Americans and the lives of countless more Allied soldiers and civilians.

The U.S. national debt rose to $4 trillion, forcing the country into debtor-nation status for the first time in seventy years. America's economic infrastructure took it on the chin. Highways and bridges fell into disrepair. Money that would normally find its way into investments in the national economy—education, job training, nonmilitary research and development—instead was diverted to the arms race and hot wars.

Perhaps the most damaging effect of the Cold War lay in the immeasurable psychological harm done to the human psyche on both sides of the iron curtain. To all those who lived through the Cold War, the threat of "the bomb" was real and pervasive. So where were the winners? The distinguished statesman George F. Kennan disclaims any such notion:

> Nobody "won" the Cold War. It was a long and costly political rivalry, fueled on both sides by unreal and exaggerated estimates of the intentions and strength of the other side. It greatly overstrained the economic resources of both countries, leaving them both, by the end of the 1980s, confronted with heavy financial, social, and—in the case of the Russians—political

problems neither had anticipated and for which neither was fully prepared. The fact that in Russia's case these changes were long desired on principle by most of us does not alter the fact that they came, and came far too precipitately, upon a population little prepared for them, thus creating new problems of the greatest seriousness for Russia, her neighbors, and the rest of us—problems to which, as yet, none of us have found effective answers.[77]

The continuing search for answers to these problems and for ways for all nations to peacefully coexist constitute humankind's best hope for survival on an ever-shrinking and increasingly dangerous planet. War is no longer an option, for there will be no winners in World War III.

Notes

Chapter 1: The Cold War

1. Quoted in Paul Johnson, *Modern Times: From the Twenties to the Nineties*. Rev. ed. New York: HarperCollins, 1991, pp. 437–38.
2. George F. Kennan, *At a Century's Ending: Reflections, 1982–1995*. Boston: Little, Brown, 1996, p. 152.
3. Quoted in Johnson, *Modern Times*, p. 435.
4. Quoted in Johnson, *Modern Times*, p. 435.
5. Quoted in Johnson, *Modern Times*, p. 436.
6. Quoted in Martin Walker, *The Cold War: A History*. New York: Holt, 1995, p. 49.
7. Quoted in Ronald E. Powaski, *The Cold War: The United States and the Soviet Union, 1917–1991*. New York: Oxford University Press, 1998, p. 72.
8. Quoted in Thomas Parrish, *The Cold War Encyclopedia*. New York: Holt, 1995, p. 208.
9. Quoted in Ronald Grigor Suny, *The Soviet Experiment: Russia, the USSR, and the Successor States*. New York: Oxford University Press, 1998, p. 360.
10. Quoted in J. M. Roberts, *The New World Order*, vol. 10, *The Illustrated History of the World*. New York: Oxford University Press, 1999, p. 11.
11. Quoted in Powaski, *The Cold War*, pp. 86–87.
12. Quoted in Powaski, *The Cold War*, p. 120.
13. Quoted in John Mack Faragher, ed., *The American Heritage Encyclopedia of American History*. New York: Holt, 1998, p. 592.
14. Quoted in Dino A. Brugioni, *Eyeball to Eyeball: The Inside Story of the Cuban Missile Crisis*, ed. Robert F. McCort. New York: Random House, 1991, p. 483.

15. Quoted in Suny, *The Soviet Experiment*, p. 424.

16. Quoted in Suny, *The Soviet Experiment*, p. 424.

Chapter 2: The Arms Race

17. Quoted in Dmitri Volkogonov, *Autopsy for an Empire: The Seven Leaders Who Built the Soviet Regime*, ed. and trans. Harold Shukman. New York: Free, 1998, p. 121.

18. Quoted in Volkogonov, *Autopsy for an Empire*, p. 121.

19. Quoted in Volkogonov, *Autopsy for an Empire*, p. 121.

20. Quoted in Vladislav Zubok and Constantine Pleshakov, *Inside the Kremlin's Cold War: From Stalin to Khrushchev*. Cambridge, MA: Harvard University Press, 1997, p. 44.

21. Quoted in Zubok and Pleshakov, *Inside the Kremlin's Cold War*, p. 151.

22. Quoted in Parrish, *The Cold War Encyclopedia*, p. 273.

23. Norman Friedman, *The Fifty Year War: Conflict and Strategy in the Cold War*. Annapolis, MD: Naval Institute Press, 1999, p. 198.

24. Friedman, *The Fifty Year War*, p. 231.

25. Quoted in Volkogonov, *Autopsy for an Empire*, p. 217.

26. Quoted in Paul Kennedy, *The Rise and Fall of the Great Powers: Economic Change and Military Conflict from 1500 to 2000*. New York: Vintage Books, 1989, pp. 389–90.

27. Quoted in Kennedy, *The Rise and Fall of the Great Powers*, p. 390.

28. Quoted in Parrish, *The Cold War Encyclopedia*, p. 61.

29. Quoted in Edmund Morris, *Dutch: A Memoir of Ronald Reagan*. New York: Random House, 1999, p. 478.

30. Quoted in Parrish, *The Cold War Encyclopedia*, p. 121.

Chapter 3: Communism's Basic Flaw

31. Martin Malia, *Russia Under Western Eyes: From the Bronze Horseman to the Lenin Mausoleum*. Cambridge, MA: Belknap Press of Harvard University Press, 1999, p. 294.

32. Quoted in Brian Moynahan, *The Russian Century: A Photographic History of Russia's One Hundred Years*. New York: Random House, 1994, p. 154.

33. Quoted in Moynahan, *The Russian Century*, p. 154.

34. Norman Davies, *Europe: A History*. New York: Oxford University Press, 1996, p. 961.
35. Quoted in Richard Overy, *Why the Allies Won*. New York: W. W. Norton, 1995, p. 187.
36. Quoted in Suny, *The Soviet Experiment*, p. 60.
37. Quoted in Suny, *The Soviet Experiment*, p. 62.
38. Quoted in Zubok and Pleshakov, *Inside the Kremlin's Cold War*, p. 177.
39. Quoted in Volkogonov, *Autopsy for an Empire*, p. 207.
40. Tim McDaniel, *The Agony of the Russian Idea*. Princeton, NJ: Princeton University Press, 1996, p. 131.
41. Quoted in Davies, *Europe*, p. 1092.
42. Quoted in Volkogonov, *Autopsy for an Empire*, p. 321.
43. Volkogonov, *Autopsy for an Empire*, p. 328.

Chapter 4: Soviet Dissent

44 Quoted in Christopher Andrew and Vasili Mitrokhin, *The Sword and the Shield: The Mitrokhin Archive and the Secret History of the KGB*. New York: BasicBooks, 1999, p. 312.
45. Quoted in Andrew and Mitrokhin, *The Sword and the Shield*, p. 312.
46. Quoted in David Remnick, *Resurrection: The Struggle for a New Russia*. New York: Vintage Books, 1998, p. 237.
47. Quoted in Parrish, *The Cold War Encyclopedia*, p. 279.
48. Quoted in Suny, *The Soviet Experiment*, p. 432.
49. Quoted in Gregory L. Freeze, ed., *Russia: A History*. New York: Oxford University Press, 1997, p. 380.
50. Quoted in David Remnick, *Lenin's Tomb: The Last Days of the Soviet Empire*. New York: Vintage Books, 1994, p. 163.
51. Quoted in Remnick, *Lenin's Tomb*, p. 164.
52. Quoted in Geoffrey Stern, ed., *Atlas of Communism*. New York: Macmillan, 1991, p. 212.
53. Mikhail Gorbachev, *Gorbachev: On My Country and the World*, trans. George Shriver. New York: Columbia University Press, 2000, p. 86.
54. Gorbachev, *Gorbachev: On My Country and the World*, p. 91.
55. Quoted in Scott Shane, *Dismantling Utopia: How Information Ended the Soviet Union*. Chicago: Elephant Paperback, 1994, pp. 242–43.

56. Suny, *The Soviet Experiment*, p. 465.

Chapter 5: Glasnost and Perestroika

57. Quoted in Michael Dobbs, *Down with Big Brother: The Fall of the Soviet Empire*. New York: Vintage Books, 1998, p. 449.
58. Quoted in Parrish, *The Cold War Encyclopedia*, p. 121.
59. Quoted in Volkogonov, *Autopsy for an Empire*, p. 442.
60. Gorbachev, *Gorbachev: On My Country and the World*, pp. 60–61.
61. Volkogonov, *Autopsy for an Empire*, p. 468.
62. Quoted in Shane, *Dismantling Utopia*, p. 137.
63. Quoted in Morris, *Dutch*, p. 635.
64. Quoted in Walker, *The Cold War*, p. 283.
65. Volkogonov, *Autopsy for an Empire*, p. 362.
66. Quoted in Morris, *Dutch*, p. 624.
67. Quoted in Parrish, *The Cold War Encyclopedia*, p. 460.
68. Quoted in Moynahan, *The Russian Century*, p. 292.
69. Quoted in Moynahan, *The Russian Century*, p. 292.
70. Quoted in Moynahan, *The Russian Century*, p. 293.
71. Quoted in Moynahan, *The Russian Century*, p. 293.
72. Gorbachev, *Gorbachev: On My Country and the World*, p. 104.
73. Quoted in Remnick, *Lenin's Tomb*, p. 389.
74. Quoted in Suny, *The Soviet Experiment*, p. 479.
75. Quoted in Moynahan, *The Russian Century*, p. 301.

Epilogue: A War Without Winners

76. Quoted in Powaski, *The Cold War*, p. 292.
77. Kennan, *At a Century's Ending*, pp. 186–87.

Chronology

1917
November 7: Bolsheviks seize power in Russia.

1942
November 6: NKVD chief Lavrenty Beria informs Soviet premier Joseph Stalin of atomic research by Western powers.

1945
February 4–12: Yalta Conference; meeting of President Franklin D. Roosevelt of the United States, Prime Minister Winston Churchill of Great Britain, and Premier Joseph Stalin of the Soviet Union.

March 23: Soviet foreign minister Vyacheslav Molotov announces that elections in Poland will be conducted Soviet-style.

April 12: President Roosevelt dies; Vice President Harry S. Truman succeeds him.

June 26: Signing of the United Nations (UN) Charter.

July 17–August 2: Potsdam Conference; meeting of President Harry S. Truman of the United States, Prime Minister Winston Churchill of Great Britain (succeeded by new prime minister Clement Attlee on July 28), and Premier Joseph Stalin of the Soviet Union.

August 6: The United States drops an atomic bomb on Hiroshima and a second bomb on Nagasaki three days later.

August 8: The Soviet Union enters the war against Japan.

September 2: Japan formally surrenders to the Allied powers, ending World War II.

October 24: United Nations Day (ratified UN Charter becomes effective).

1946

January 5: A letter from U.S. president Harry S. Truman to U.S. secretary of state James F. Byrnes marks the point of departure of U.S. policy toward the USSR.

March 5: British statesman Winston Churchill serves notice of an "iron curtain" in Europe during an address at Westminster College in Fulton, Missouri, lending formal public recognition to the Cold War.

1947

February 21: Britain informs the United States that it will be forced to stop aid to Greece and Turkey on March 31.

March 12: President Truman commits the United States to supporting the free peoples of the world without limits of time or place; his vows become known as the Truman Doctrine.

1948

June 5: The Marshall Plan (European Recovery Plan) is announced at Harvard University.

June 18: Western powers introduce a new deutsche mark into their occupation zones in Germany.

June 23: Soviets issue their own new mark in their German occupation zone.

June 24, 1948–May 5, 1949: Berlin blockade and airlift takes place.

1949

April 4: North Atlantic Treaty Organization (NATO) is formed.

May 23: Federal Republic of Germany (West Germany) is founded.

August 29: Soviet scientists successfully detonate a nuclear device.

October 7: German Democratic Republic (East Germany) is created.

1950

June 25: North Korean forces invade South Korea; the Korean War begins.

1952

November 1: U.S. scientists conduct the first successful test of a hydrogen (fusion) bomb at Enewetak Atoll in the western Pacific Ocean.

November 4: General Dwight D. Eisenhower is elected U.S. president.

1953

March 5: Soviet premier Joseph Stalin dies.

June 19: Julius and Ethel Rosenberg are executed for providing the Soviets with U.S. nuclear secrets.

July 27: Cease-fire agreement is signed in Korea.

1955

November 9: Soviets detonate their first hydrogen bomb.

1956

July 19–December 4: Suez Crisis; Egypt nationalizes the Suez Canal when the United States withdraws financial support for the Aswan Dam.

1957

January 5: President Eisenhower declares that the United States will defend Middle Eastern nations against Communist aggression; his declaration becomes known as the Eisenhower Doctrine.

October 4: Soviets launch *Sputnik I*, the world's first artificial satellite.

1959

April 4: President Eisenhower commits the United States to maintaining South Vietnam as a separate national state, effectively marking the start of U.S. involvement in Vietnam.

July 8: The first American servicemen (military advisers) are killed in Vietcong attack on Bien Hoa, South Vietnam.

1960

November 8: John F. Kennedy is elected president of the United States.

1962

October 14–November 7: Cuban Missile Crisis; U.S.-Soviet confrontation over the installation of Soviet missiles in Cuba.

1963

August 5: The United States, Great Britain, and the Soviet Union sign the Nuclear Test Ban Treaty of 1963.

November 22: President Kennedy is assassinated in Dallas; Vice President Lyndon B. Johnson succeeds him.

1972

May 26: U.S. president Richard M. Nixon and Soviet premier Aleksey Kosygin sign the SALT I (Strategic Arms Limitation Treaty I) agreement in Moscow.

1973

December 31: The size of the U.S. military contingent in Vietnam is limited to fifty.

1975

April 30: Vietnam War ends.

1979

December 27: Soviet forces invade Afghanistan to back Marxist government.

1985

March 11: Mikhail Gorbachev is elected Soviet general secretary.

1987

June 12: U.S. president Ronald Reagan implores Soviet president Mikhail Gorbachev to tear down the Berlin Wall.

1988

May 31: U.S. president Ronald Reagan addresses students at Moscow University during summit meeting with Soviet president Mikhail Gorbachev.

June 28: Nineteenth Conference of the Communist Party of the Soviet Union convenes in Moscow.

October 1: Soviet general secretary Mikhail Gorbachev is elected Soviet president and chief of state.

1989

February 15: Last Soviet troops leave Afghanistan.
November 9: The Berlin Wall is breached.

1991

January 22: Gorbachev denies any role in the Vilnius revolt.

March 17: Soviet citizens approve Gorbachev's referendum aimed at preserving the Soviet Union.

June 12: Boris Yeltsin wins election as president of the new Russian Federation.

July 29: U.S. president George Bush and Soviet president Mikhail Gorbachev sign Strategic Arms Reduction Treaty (START) in Moscow.

August 19–22: Attempted coup against Gorbachev fails.

December 8: Russia, Ukraine, and Belarus sign an agreement creating the Commonwealth of Independent States (CIS) as the successor to the Soviet Union.

December 25: Soviet president and chief of state Mikhail Gorbachev resigns, marking the dissolution of the Soviet Union and the collapse of communism in Europe.

Glossary

ABM: Antiballistic missile.

ALCM: Air-launched cruise missile.

atomic bomb: A bomb that derives its immense explosive power through **fission**.

Basic Principles Agreement: A code of international conduct for nations, mutually agreed to by the United States and the Soviet Union in Moscow in 1972.

Berlin blockade and airlift: The Soviet blockade of Berlin in 1946–1947, which was rendered ineffective by a massive airlift by Western powers.

Bolsheviks: Majority members of the Russian Social Democratic Party led by Vladimir Lenin; revolutionists who overthrew the czarist government of Russia and seized power on November 7, 1917; *Bolsheviki*, in Russian.

bourgeois: A member of the middle class.

bourgeoisie: The middle class.

capitalism: An economic system in which trade and industry are controlled by private owners; a free-enterprise system. Compare with **communism**.

Cold War: Phrase coined in 1947 by journalist Herbert Bayard Swope, in a speech written for financier and presidential adviser Bernard Baruch, to identify the post–1945 political, economic, strategic, and military conflict between the Western Allies—headed by the United States—and the Soviet Union and other Communist nations.

collectivization: State ownership or control of production and distribution, as collective farms and farming.

communism: A social system in which property is owned by the community or state and each member works for the benefit of all; Communism (with an uppercase *C*): a political doctrine or movement that seeks to overthrow **capitalism** and establish a form of communism in its place.

Cuban Missile Crisis: U.S.-Soviet confrontation over the installation of Soviet missiles in Cuba in 1962.

de-Stalinization: The discrediting of Stalin, primarily during the Khrushchev regime.

détente: An interval of relaxed tensions, especially between nations.

dialectic: The logical examination of an idea.

Eisenhower Doctrine: President Eisenhower's declaration that the United States would defend Middle Eastern nations against Communist aggression.

fission: The division (splitting) of a heavy atomic nucleus that produces a release of energy.

fusion: The union of atomic nuclei to form a heavier nucleus that produces a release of energy.

glasnost: Soviet policy of the 1980s allowing open dicussion of the nation's social and economic problems and freer dissemination of news and information.

H-bomb: A bomb that derives its enormous explosive power through **fusion**.

Helsinki Accords: Agreements between most of the major Western powers and the Soviet Union in 1975 to accept the postwar Eastern European national boundaries as permanent.

ICBM: Intercontinental ballistic missile.

IRBM: Intermediate-range ballistic missile.

iron curtain: Phrase originated by British statesman Winston Churchill, symbolizing an unseen barrier of secrecy and censorship isolating the Soviet Union and its Communist satellites after World War II.

KGB: State Security Committee (Russian: Komitet Gosudarstvennoi Bezopasnosti); the Soviet agency responsible for internal security, intelligence gathering, foreign operations, and border control; established in 1954.

kulaks: Profiteering peasant farmers.

Marshall Plan: European Recovery Plan; a U.S. program that provided $10.2 billion in postwar economic aid to help rehabilitate twenty-two European nations.

Marxism: The economic and social philosophy of Karl Marx and Friedrich Engels.

military-industrial complex: Phrase originated by President Eisenhower to describe the coalition of politicians, defense contractors, and military officials whose power unduly influences U.S. policies and practices.

MIRV: Multiple independently targetable reentry vehicle.

missile gap: The mistaken belief (circa 1960) that the Eisenhower administration had allowed the United States to lag far behind the Soviet Union in the development and deployment of strategic missiles; actually, the Americans held an overwhelming lead over the Soviets.

NATO: North Atlantic Treaty Organization; a defensive alliance formed on April 4, 1949, whose original members comprised the United States, Canada, and the Western European nations, excluding Sweden, Spain, and Switzerland.

neutron: An uncharged element present in all known atomic nuclei except the hydrogen nucleus.

NEP: New Economic Policy; economic program introduced by Vladimir Lenin after the Russian Revolution of 1917 to help bridge the gap between **capitalism** and **socialism**.

neo-Stalinist: A new, latter-day advocate of Stalin and his policies.

Nepmen: Traders in scarce goods under Lenin's New Economic Policy.

NKVD: People's Commissariat for Internal Affairs (Russian: Narodnyi Komissariat Vnutrennykh Dyel); the Soviet agency responsible for state security from 1934 to 1943; a forerunner to the **KGB**.

nucleus: The positively charged central portion of an atom.

peaceful coexistence: A phrase often associated with Nikita Khrushchev (but originating with Lenin) that implies the need of competing systems of governments to work together in peace and harmony.

perestroika: Soviet policy of economic and governmental reform initiated in the 1980s.

petty-bourgeoisie: The lower middle class.

plutonium: A radioactive chemical element used in nuclear reactors and weapons.

Politburo: Political bureau; the principal policy-making and executive committee of the Soviet Communist Party.

proletariat: The working class.

SALT: Strategic Arms Limitations Talks (either I or II).

samizdat: Literally, "self-published," as opposed to *gozidat,* or "state-published"; name applied to underground political publications.

SDI: Strategic Defense Initiative, often called "Star Wars"; a U.S. missile-defense program (circa 1983) aimed at creating a great defensive shield that would intercept and destroy incoming enemy missiles.

SLCM: Sea-launched cruise missile.

socialism: A general term for the political and economic theory advocating collective or state ownership and management of the means for the production and distribution of goods.

Sputnik I: The world's first artificial satellite, orbited by the Soviet Union on October 4, 1957.

START: Strategic Arms Reduction Treaty.

Truman Doctrine: President Truman's commitment to support free peoples of the world against forced subjugation, with no limitations of time or place.

uranium: A heavy gray metallic element used as a source of nuclear energy.

USSR: Union of Soviet Socialist Republics; the Soviet Union.

Yalta Conference: World War II meeting of U.S. president Franklin D. Roosevelt, British prime minister Winston Churchill, and Soviet premier Joseph Stalin; the meeting was held in the Crimean resort town of Yalta (February 4–12, 1945), chiefly to plan the postwar division and occupation of Europe.

For Further Reading

Kai Bird, *The Color of Truth: McGeorge Bundy and William Bundy: Brothers in Arms*. New York: Simon & Schuster, 1998. The definitive biography of the Bundy brothers, who advised presidents about peace and war during the most dangerous days of the Cold War.

H. W. Brands, *The Devil We Knew: Americans and the Cold War*. New York: Oxford University Press, 1993. An examination of the American experience during the Cold War, from the immediate aftermath of World War II through the disintegration of the Soviet Union.

Ariel Cohen, *Russian Imperialism: Development and Crisis*. Westport, CT: Praeger, 1998. A close scrutiny of the collapse of the Soviet Union and what it means to the Russian people and the world at large.

Richard M. Fried, *The Russians Are Coming! The Russians Are Coming!: Pageantry and Patriotism in Cold-War America*. New York: Oxford University Press, 1998. The American scene during the McCarthy era of the Cold War.

J. A. S. Grenville, *A History of the World in the Twentieth Century*. Cambridge, MA: Harvard University Press, 1994. A masterful study of the significant events of the twentieth century, including the Cold War.

Paul Johnson, *A History of the American People*. New York: HarperCollins, 1997. A masterly treatise on Americans and their national experience, from 1580 to the 1990s.

Lionel Kochan and John Keep, *The Making of Modern Russia*. 3rd ed. New York: Penguin, 1998. A recently updated one-volume history of Russia from the sixth century to the present.

Ernest R. May and Philip D. Zelikow, eds., *The Kennedy Tapes: Inside the White House During the Cuban Missile Crisis*. Cambridge, MA: Belknap Press of Harvard University Press, 1997. The taped inside story of the critical U.S.-Soviet deliberations that might have changed the face of the world.

William E. Odom, *The Collapse of the Soviet Military*. New Haven, CT: Yale University Press, 1998. A distinguished U.S. Army officer and scholar traces the rise and fall of the Soviet military.

Norman Polmar et al., *Chronology of the Cold War at Sea, 1945–1991*. Annapolis, MD: Naval Institute Press, 1997. Discusses Cold War developments at sea and events related to U.S. and Soviet naval forces and their allies.

Robert Service, *A History of Twentieth-Century Russia*. Cambridge, MA: Harvard University Press, 1997. Analyzes the odd mixture of political, economic, and social elements that constituted the Soviet formula.

Dmitri K. Simes, *After the Collapse: Russia Seeks Its Place as a Great Power*. New York: Simon & Schuster, 1999. An insightful examination of the ongoing adversarial relationship between the United States and Russia.

Charles Townshend, ed., *The Oxford Illustrated History of Modern War*. New York: Oxford University Press, 1997. An authoritative history of modern warfare, including an illuminating chapter on the Cold War.

David C. Turnley, *The Russian Heart: Days of Crisis and Hope*. New York: Aperture Foundation, 1992. A photographic journal capturing the people and events of the second Russian revolution.

Works Consulted

Christopher Andrew and Vasili Mitrokhin, *The Sword and the Shield: The Mitrokhin Archive and the Secret History of the KGB.* New York: BasicBooks, 1999. An unprecedented look at Soviet foreign intelligence activities drawn from almost thirty years of KGB files.

Dino A. Brugioni, *Eyeball to Eyeball: The Inside Story of the Cuban Missile Crisis.* Ed. by Robert F. McCort. New York: Random House, 1991. The definitive account of the Cuban Missile Crisis by an eyewitness member of the intelligence community.

Brian Crozier, *The Rise and Fall of the Soviet Empire.* Rocklin, CA: Forum, 1999. The brutal history of the Soviet empire—its birth, life, and sudden death.

Norman Davies, *Europe: A History.* New York: Oxford University Press, 1996. A monumental intellectual achievement in the scope, analysis, and expression of European history; excellent coverage of the Cold War.

Carlo D'Este, *Patton: A Genius for War.* New York: HarperCollins, 1995. A revealing portrait of a complex and controversial military personality.

Michael Dobbs, *Down with Big Brother: The Fall of the Soviet Empire.* New York: Vintage Books, 1998. An eyewitness report on the collapse of communism and the downfall of the Soviet Union.

John Mack Faragher, ed., *The American Heritage Encyclopedia of American History.* New York: Holt, 1998. A remarkable one-volume representation of America's past.

Gregory L. Freeze, ed., *Russia: A History.* New York: Oxford University Press, 1997. A major history of Russia from its Kievan origins to the early Yeltsin years.

Norman Friedman, *The Fifty Year War: Conflict and Strategy in the Cold War.* Annapolis, MD: Naval Institute Press, 1999. A comprehensive, incisive, and provocative analysis of the Cold War from the Soviet Union's involvement in the Spanish Civil War to its dissolution on Christmas Day 1991.

Mikhail Gorbachev, *Gorbachev: On My Country and the World*. Trans. George Shriver. New York: Columbia University Press, 2000. The whole sweep of the Soviet experiment as told by its last steward.

Paul Johnson, *Modern Times: From the Twenties to the Nineties*. Rev. ed. New York: HarperCollins, 1991. A major analysis on how the modern age came into being and where it is heading; valuable Cold War coverage.

George F. Kennan, *At a Century's Ending: Reflections, 1982–1995*. Boston: Little, Brown, 1996. Reflections on the political and military forces, particularly during the Cold War, that have characterized the postwar world.

Paul Kennedy, *The Rise and Fall of the Great Powers: Economic Change and Military Conflict from 1500 to 2000*. New York: Vintage Books, 1989. A bold and lucid treatise on current economic and political dilemmas viewed from the perspective of world history.

Martin Malia, *Russia Under Western Eyes: From the Bronze Horseman to the Lenin Mausoleum*. Cambridge, MA: Belknap Press of Harvard University Press, 1999. A sweeping view of Russia seen not as a barbarian menace but as an outermost member of the European community.

Karl Marx and Friedrich Engels, "Manifesto of the Communist Party," trans. Samuel Moore and ed. Friedrich Engels, in Robert Maynard Hutchins, ed., *Great Books of the Western World*. Vol. 50. *Marx*. Chicago: University of Chicago Press, 1952. The classic treatise on communism by Marx and Engels.

Tim McDaniel, *The Agony of the Russian Idea*. Princeton, NJ: Princeton University Press, 1996. Examines the inability of Russian leaders over the last two hundred years to create the foundations of a viable modern society.

Edmund Morris, *Dutch: A Memoir of Ronald Reagan*. New York: Random House, 1999. An in-depth study of the former president, including his role in the Cold War.

Brian Moynahan, *The Russian Century: A Photographic History of Russia's One Hundred Years*. New York: Random House, 1994. A photographic tapestry of Russia, from the last days of the czars to the collapse of the Soviet Union.

Richard Overy, *Why the Allies Won*. New York: W. W. Norton, 1995.

An examination of some of the deeper factors affecting military success and failure in World War II.

Thomas Parrish, *The Cold War Encyclopedia*. New York: Holt, 1995. A chronology of events and a dictionary of terms, people, and places relating to the Cold War.

Ronald E. Powaski, *The Cold War: The United States and the Soviet Union, 1917–1991*. New York: Oxford University Press, 1998. Covers the major issues of the protracted struggle in a highly readable format.

David Remnick, *Lenin's Tomb: The Last Days of the Soviet Empire*. New York: Vintage Books, 1994. A fast-paced account of the demise of the Soviet Union.

————, *Resurrection: The Struggle for a New Russia*. New York: Vintage Books, 1998. A stirring chronicle of the new Russia emerging from the ashes and rubble of the collapsed Soviet Union.

J. M. Roberts, *The New World Order*. Vol. 10. *The Illustrated History of the World*. New York: Oxford University Press, 1999. The evolving shape of the world through the tumultuous Cold War years to its current state.

Scott Shane, *Dismantling Utopia: How Information Ended the Soviet Union*. Chicago: Elephant Paperback, 1994. How the removal of information controls drove the Soviet system to ruin.

Geoffrey Stern, ed., *Atlas of Communism*. New York: Macmillan, 1991. Traces the legacy and progress of communism from Karl Marx to Boris Yeltsin.

Ronald Grigor Suny, *The Soviet Experiment: Russia, the USSR, and the Successor States*. New York: Oxford University Press, 1998. A gripping narrative of the Soviets from the last czar of the Russian empire to the first president of the Russian republic.

Dmitri Volkogonov, *Autopsy for an Empire: The Seven Leaders Who Built the Soviet Regime*. Ed. and trans. Harold Shukman. New York: Free, 1998. The breakup of the Soviet Union told through the profiles of its seven leaders.

Martin Walker, *The Cold War: A History*. New York: Holt, 1995. A major study of this important era for the general reader.

Vladislav Zubok and Constantine Pleshakov, *Inside the Kremlin's Cold War: From Stalin to Khrushchev*. Cambridge, MA: Harvard University Press, 1997. A major interpretation of the Cold War from the Soviet perspective.

Index

Picture Credits

Cover: © Lewis Fineman/FPG International
AP/Wide World Photos, 34
Archive France/Archive Photos, 26
Archive Photos, 25, 45, 48, 57, 61
© Bettmann/Corbis, 17, 22, 24, 29, 43, 51, 53
Camera Press Ltd./Archive Photos, 40
Express Newspapers/Archive Photos, 76
Express Newspapers/D377/Archive Photos, 54
© Hulton-Deutsch Collection/Corbis, 12
Hulton Getty/Liaison Agency, 35, 38
© Marc Garanger/Corbis, 63
Imperial War Museum/Archive Photos, 10
Lambert/Archive Photos, 32
© Wally McNamee/Corbis, 7
© Reuters/David Brauchli/Archive Photos, 78
© Reuters/Viktor Korotayev/Archive Photos, 80
© Reuters/Alexander Natruskin/Archive Photos, 59
© Reuters Newmedia, Inc./Corbis, 69
© Peter Turnley/Corbis, 66, 73, 79, 82, 85
U.S. Army/Courtesy Harry S. Truman Library, 13

About the Author

After serving nine years with the U.S. Marine Corps, Earle Rice Jr. attended San Jose City College and Foothill College on the San Francisco peninsula.

He has authored more than thirty books for young adults, including fast-action fiction and adaptations of *Dracula, All Quiet on the Western Front,* and *The Grapes of Wrath.* Mr. Rice has written twenty-one books for Lucent, including *The Cuban Revolution, The Nuremberg Trials, The Final Solution, Nazi War Criminals, The Third Reich, Kamikazes*, and seven books in the popular Great Battles series. He has also written articles, short stories, and miscellaneous website materials, and he has previously worked for several years as a technical writer.

Mr. Rice is a former senior design engineer in the aerospace industry who now devotes full time to his writing. The author is a member of the Society of Children's Book Writers and Illustrators; the League of World War I Aviation Historians and its UK-based sister organization, Cross and Cockade International; the United States Naval Institute; and the Air Force Association. He lives in Julian, California, with his wife, daughter, two granddaughters, and two cats.